Fish, Timber, Granite & Gold

Fish, Timber, Granite & Gold

Researched by
Peter Bergholtz
& Donald Dawson

Written by Eleanor Parsons

Printed in the United States of America
By DS Graphics, 120 Steadman St, Lowell, MA 01851

ISBN 0-97460-51-0-7

Sponsored by the Sandy Bay Historical Society and Museums
Rockport, MA

Book & Cover Design by Leslie D. Bartlett
Cover Image : 'The Great Wall Realized'

THE OLD STONE WALLS.

...

Mile after mile of gray stone wall
Are left until our day;
But the active, busy builders,
We wonder who were they?
Moss-grown, their work is left behind,—
'Twas neatly done and well;
But years ago the builders
Vanished from hill and dell.

Essex. S.S. Bartlett

— *The Essex Antiquarian* , 1897 —

TABLE OF CONTENTS

Acknowledgements

The idea for this book evolved from the minds of Peter Bergholtz and Donald Dawson, first merely as a matter of curiosity and then as a full-fledged idea. But the best of ideas must call upon the best of help and, along with author Eleanor Parsons, they acknowledge with profound gratitude the assistance they have received along the way.

Leslie Bartlett, photographer, designer and editor, with his enthusiasm and his wonderfully creative ideas, not only provided for the internal layout and the cover design but his matchless skills in text and figures enabled him to enhance the production into a print-ready format.

Cynthia Peckham, Curator of The Sandy Bay Historical Society and Museums, with research facilities and her extensive knowledge of Cape Ann history, was endlessly helpful and generous with her time and suggestions. This book would not have been possible without her help.

Mary Sibbalds, as President of the Sandy Bay Historical Society, provided valuable assistance with her expert genealogical research.

Ellen Nelson, assistant at the Cape Ann Historical Association in Gloucester, helped in researching early deeds and in locating reference books.

Volunteers of the Gloucester City Hall Archives Committee were equally as helpful in the researching of selectmen's records and other early documents.

Michael Comeau, as Head Archivist of the Massachusetts Archives at Columbia Point, provided research suggestions and access to the General Records of the Treasurer-Receiver. These were the earliest records of the American Colonies, beginning in 1775, an invaluable source of reference.

There were many helpful people at the Salem Registry of Deeds and at the Phillips Library of the Peabody- Essex Museum. ROBERT LANPHER of the North Attleboro Historical Society and MARION WRIGHTMAN of the Attleboro Historical Society both provided valuable information on the history of the area.

Near the end of the project, ANNE GRADY, Architectural Historian and Preservation Consultant, assisted in analysis of the structure of the Garrison House as one of the earliest houses on Cape Ann, a study that is still going on.

A special thanks must go to PATRICIA DAWSON, wife of Donald Dawson, for her meticulous reading of the manuscript for corrections, omissions and clarifications.

A special thanks, too, to A.A. PARADIS, retired editor and publisher, for his tireless pursuit of errors and proper construction of the manuscript, as well as his expert advice.

Words of appreciation reach across the Atlantic Ocean to ERIC MILLER, Author, Historian, and a founder of the Leckhampton Local Historical Society, Leckhampton, Gloucestershire, England, for sharing opinions and research sources concerning the English roots of the Norwood family and their ancestral home, Leckhampton Court, and for permission to use illustrations from his own publication, *Leckhampton Court Manor House to Hospice*.

Seated: Eleanor Parsons,
Standing: (l to r), Donald Dawson, Peter Bergholtz

About the Authors

Peter Bergholtz, a native of Reading, Massachusetts, holds a BA degree from Bowdoin College and an MBA from Dartmouth. After twelve years of employment with the New England Telephone Company he established his own manufacturing company, Ken-Bar, Inc. In a business career spanning forty years he has owned and operated two other companies, has served as president of several industrial organizations, and has obtained three patents. While remaining active as CEO of Ken-Bar, Inc. he serves on several community boards in Rockport, where he lives with his wife, Joyce.

Donald Dawson, M.D., born in Milwaukee, Wisconsin, holds degrees from Lawrence College, George Washington University, and Georgetown University, with surgical training at the University of Chicago. His medical career, spanning forty years, includes affiliation with foreign institutions, as well as surgeon and medical administrator in mental health and developmental disabilities in Michigan. He has published many research papers and served as Director of Medical Programs at Eunice Shriver Center, Waltham, Mass. Dr. Dawson currently serves as a medical program consultant. He lives in Rockport with his wife, Patricia.

Eleanor Parsons, a former teacher in Maine and Rockport, attended Farmington and the University of Maine. After marriage to Rockport native, Story Parsons, her fascination with the myths, legends and the living history of Cape Ann lured her from teaching to writing, and she qualified as a member of the National League of American Pen Women. She has published numerous articles and five books; *Hannah and the Hatchet Gang*; *Thachers Island of the Twin Lights*; *Nippers, Nightcaps, and Needles*; *Rockport, The Making of a Tourist Treasure*; and *A Town Called Drew*. This most recent book, *Fish, Timber, Granite & Gold*, was written in cooperation with her two inspiring researchers.

Figures

Plated Maps (following page 36)

Sources

Unless otherwise noted, all figures, illustrations and maps are from the archives of the Sandy Bay Historical Society and Museums, Rockport, MA.

Additional Sources

LB (Leslie Bartlett)

PB (Peter Bergholtz)

DD (Donald Dawson)

SH (Susan Holden)

EM (Eric Miller)

MSA (Massachusetts State Archives)

MN (Maureen Norwood)

EP (Eleanor Parsons)

A Great Stone Wall on Cape Ann Leads to the Story of the Early Norwoods

Figure 1. Old Wall at Rockport's Headlands

• • •

The Norwood Legacy

• • •

Stone walls have attracted the eyes of travelers in the New England countryside for over 200 years. Though some pass by the walls with little thought, it has been estimated that half a million miles of stone walls edge the fields and woodlands of New England. In his book, "Stone by Stone," Robert M.Thorson calls attention to the importance of stone walls and the stories they have to tell.

"Man cannot live without walls, without boundaries, without limits," said poet Robert Frost. Some say they hear music in the stones, while others, the artists among us, find beauty in their colors and shapes and structure. Shakespeare told us there were sermons in stones.

But for Donald Dawson and Peter Bergholtz it was curiosity that sent them on a quest to solve the mystery of the Great Stone Wall that outlined one side of Peter's property. Don and Peter, two men living in the same community, had never met until their curiosity about the wall brought them together. They paced the stone structure from one end to the other, and measured the length to be 2000 feet. At first it was the size of the stones that drew their attention. Some, they observed, had a circumference of six feet or more, not the usual size for construction of New England stone walls. In some sections, they noticed, the wall rose as high as eight feet, with immense boulders placed on the top. "Why build the wall so high, and with such enormous stones?" they asked each other. "Where did the stones come from and how were they moved? When was the wall built?" One question followed another, and then the inevitable and persistent question arose,

"Who built this Great Stone Wall?"

Their search for answers led Don and Peter far beyond their first idle curiosity. It was to take them to the archives of the Sandy Bay Historical Society and Museums [SBHS], to Gloucester's City Hall archives, then on to Salem and Boston, to records of patriots, pirates, and privateers of the American Revolution, to early fishermen and farmers who had lived in the area, to the romance of young Susanna Norwood, to the building of her own house of stone, and even down the trail of the legendary cache of pirate gold.

Not long into their search, it became apparent to Don and Peter that this one stone wall had a story to tell, a story that began in Olde England but began to unfold in New England. They listened to the story the Great Stone Wall had to tell them.

•••

ENGLISH ORIGIN • GOOSE COVE• WITCH HOUSE

•••

The boat carrying twenty-year-old Francis Norwood from Gloucester, England, to Gloucester, Massachusetts, in 1657, is believed to have landed first at Saugus. Some historians say the voyage came to an end at Lynn, but the two communities were as one some twenty years earlier, and it is known that vessels of thirty or forty tons regularly sailed over the salt water flats of Saugus at high tide. Records show that many vessels of those days were seeking refuge at Barbados, an island of the British West Indies, but whether Francis actually sailed that route remains unclear. Researchers cannot overlook the fact, however, that during that same year, 1657, the British Parliament sent a fleet to Barbados to quell a disturbance there. At that time a trade agreement was being worked out, but while awaiting orders from King Charles II, the fleet sat idly by for ten weeks, finally setting sail for Virginia and New England. At this same time, historians have noted, Captain Elias Hasket Derby, a prosperous merchant and sea captain from Salem, Massachusetts, was named a temporary governor of Barbados. During this period of unrest, both political and religious, according to British Historian Eric Miller, many young men sailed to America seeking adventure or fortune. The intriguing question remains unanswered as to whether Francis Norwood and his companions stopped at this British Island and may have been influenced by Elias Hasket Derby and his profitable shipping interests, to set their sails for the Massachusetts coast.

Although the salt flats of Saugus were viewed as dangerous for navigators at low tide, with perilous breakers and rocks that required skillful pilots, for the same reasons the region was considered to be well protected from approaching hostile ships. In constant use, the British travelers discovered, were canoe-like water transports, called dugouts. These canoes, no more than floating logs, were hollowed out of whole pine trees, twenty feet long and two-and-a-half feet around them, and nearly every household owned one or more. As the most common means of conveyance from ship to shore, it is likely that one of these hollowed-out logs would have brought Francis Norwood from his vessel, over the salt flats, to the Massachusetts shore.

The young Norwood, probably traveling with other members of his family, had escaped from British political attempts at reform that had killed his father, Thomas, and beheaded King Charles I. Historians of the era, as well as a descendant, Maureen Norwood, in her family genealogy, have indicated that if Francis had not actually descended from royalty, his family estate had most certainly abutted the acreage of kings. The young Francis, however, sought only a safe haven from the political unrest of the Cromwell years. It is unlikely that he looked beyond his own safety, much less envisioned the Norwood dynasty that he was about to establish in America.

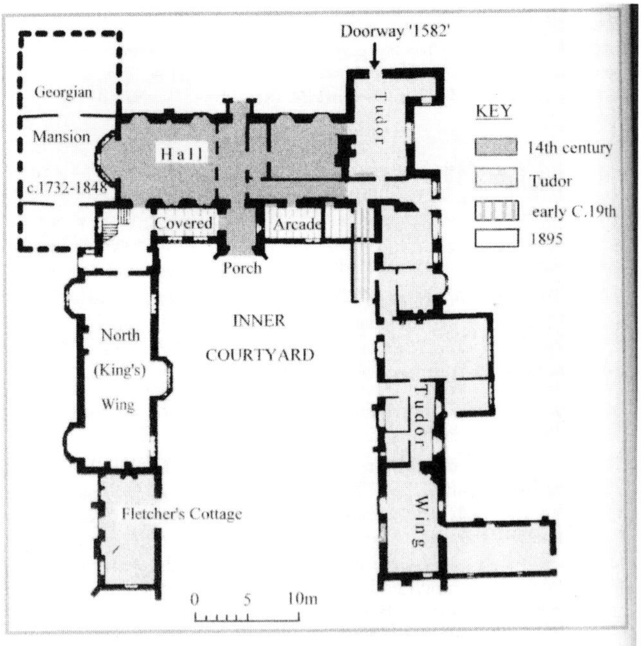

Figure 2. Plan of Leckhampton Court showing the stages of development
Based on plans in the The Architects' Journal and published in Leckhampton Court Manor House to Hospice by Eric Miller

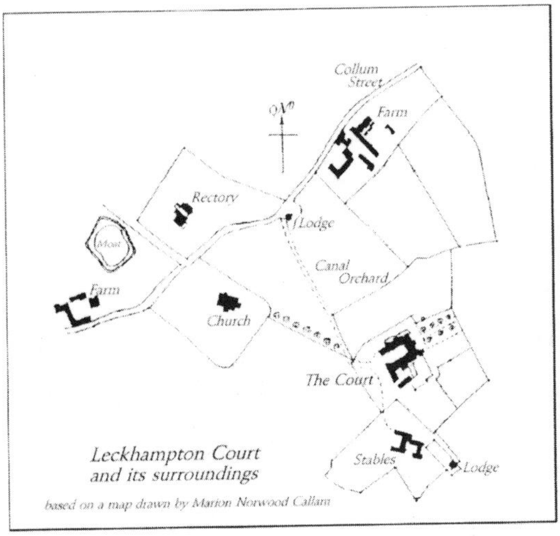

Figure 3. Leckhampton Court and its surroundings

Figure 4. Detail from a portrait of William Norwood by Cornelius Jansen

Furthermore, he could not have dreamed of the enormous influence he and his family would have on the development of Cape Ann, that portion of Massachusetts that bore the name of his British Queen.

Over several centuries in England, the Norwood name had evolved from Northwood, the name of a distinguished family known to have worked the family estate, fought in the political hostilities, and lived close to the British monarchy. John Northwood, born in 1455, had assumed possession, by way of his marriage and royal status, of a land grant of 2000 acres, in

Figure 5. Leckhampton Manor

Figure 6. An engraving of Leckhampton Court from Samuel Lyson's Collection of Gloucestershire Antiquities published in 1793

Cheltenham, near Gloucester, England. The property, Leckhampton Court, included an ancient manor house built of blocks of stone, and for the next 400 years it remained under the successive control of eleven "Lords of the Manor" Norwoods. During John Northwood's residency he proceeded to add a wing on the north end of the structure, an addition that stretched the manor house to an imposing length, but years later (in 1732) some upset coal embers burned this wing, in time to be replaced by a three-story wing of Georgian style. In another one hundred years following John's occupancy of the Manor, William Norwood was said to be the most distinguished of its occupants.

It was John's great-grandson, Thomas, born in 1618, who was killed in a battle at Taunton with Cromwell's forces as they attempted to remove Charles I from his throne. Francis Norwood, the second son in the family, then inherited Leckhampton Court. Francis and his wife had nine sons and nine daughters to support but they assumed the guardianship of the young Francis, his namesake born in 1637, the eight-year-old son of the slain Thomas. No record can be found of a marriage of Thomas or of the birth of his son. We can only assume, as does Norwood family historian, Marion Norwood Callam, that Thomas was the father of the young Francis as he later named his first son Thomas. A great deal of research by genealogists has revealed no further information and we may never know more on the subject of his parents. Then under great financial hardship, as can be imagined with such a large family, Francis sold Leckhampton Court to Henry, a brother and a bachelor. Eventually, according to the historian Eric Miller, "the estate passed in succession to the three surviving sons of Francis." The last of the Norwoods to live there, another Henry (1773-1797), was said to have obtained several mortgages to finance development of stone quarries on the property.

Meanwhile, with Charles I executed, Charles II came out of exile and regained the throne (1660) but, as a result of all this political unrest, young Francis set sail to comparative safety in America. Such adventures, incidentally, were not uncommon for prominent British families, while helping to speed up settlement in the new continent. Five of William Norwood's grandsons and one great-grandson, all related, as it happened, to the Governor of Virginia, emigrated to Virginia and Massachusetts.

Saugus was slightly west of Lynn, nine miles from Boston. The name Saugus, as interpreted from the Indian dialect, means "extended" and perhaps was suggestive of its two-and-a-half miles of salt marshes. Twenty years earlier, in 1637, after some bickering over a name, the two communities, Lynn and Saugus, had asked the General Court for a ruling on which name they should use. The decision was said to be the shortest enactment ever passed by the court: "Saugust is Lin." One hundred seventy-five years later Saugus reclaimed its original name.

Figure 7. Map of Indian Lands and Localities in Essex County Massachusetts by Sidney Perley

Along with the salt marshes, the newcomers found there "fresh meadows, good grass, lakes, ponds, and an abundance of fresh fish" within a mile of the town. The nearby Merrimac River, with a name that meant "strong" to the native Indians of the region, formed a boundary for Indian tribes of Cape Ann. The Agawam tribesmen were considered more peaceful, and more skillful as farmers, than other tribes of the Merrimac region. As the newcomers further explored the region, they reported finding a great variety of trees: "ash, walnut, cedar, aspen, and elm." In many places, though, they found the soil barren of trees and therefore suitable for plowing, where they could plant corn, barley, rye, and oats. Meanwhile, curious about the new land, and exploring the Ipswich and Merrimac Rivers in their dug-outs, they discovered even more fish and other seafoods such as mussels, clams, and lobsters along the shore. Many years later, a poetic Whittier described these tidal river mouths:

"Broad meadows reached out seaward, the tidal creeks between
And hills rolled wave-like inland, with oaks and walnuts green."

Six years elapsed before the young Francis moved on to Cape Ann, but his time in Saugus was well spent. While working at an inn owned by Clement Coldam, he met and married the innkeeper's daughter, Elizabeth. Since Gloucester was already known to British mariners, it can be assumed that Francis and his companions made exploratory trips to Cape Ann, and both the Norwood and Coldam families took over land grants there at about the same time. The usual mode of travel to Cape Ann was by water, the only other route being a rough cart trail through dense wilderness. In 1664, Francis and Elizabeth made their permanent move to Gloucester.

While Francis Norwood was not the first white man to settle at Cape Ann— small groups of fishermen had settled in Gloucester, and the Pools and Tarrs had settled at Sandy Bay—he was one of the first, along with Joseph Allen, to receive a six-acre grant, from a total of eighty-two then being allotted to all men of Cape Ann. Acceptance of the six acres required the owner to build a house there within six months. The Norwoods, the Allens, and also the Davis family, who settled on both sides of the Annisquam River, were destined to maintain close business ties and land holdings for many years to come. Gloucester records show the Norwood transaction, in almost illegible handwriting: "Given unto ffrancis Norwood att the Towne meeting, six acres of upland liing by Goose Cove."

Figure 8. The road to Francis Norwood's house at Goose Cove, Gloucester

Francis and Elizabeth took possession of their land at Goose Cove, an isolated area of Gloucester that grew at a slow pace in the next twenty-five years, while their family expanded to ten children, five sons and five daughters. The first son, born in 1664, and named Thomas after Francis Norwood's father who was lost in battle, was followed by the nine other children: Thomas 1664, Francis 1666, Elizabeth 1668, Mary 1671, Stephen 1674, Deborah 1677, Hannah 1679, Joshua 1683, Caleb 1685, Abigail 1689.

The house that Francis and Elizabeth built on their land at Goose Cove is still standing, more than three centuries later, near the stone causeway bridge. Historian James Pringle noted that Francis Norwood's home was

Figure 9. Francis Norwood's House with a sloop tied up at his pier

Figure 10. Francis Norwood's House on Goose Cove

"snugly sheathed against winter in the sea fogs in sweet-smelling pine." Two green rugs brought color out of the sea fog, and a freshly painted chest set against the wall served as a sofa. Some hand-made tables, still covered with the dust from a carpenter's shop, were placed for convenient use. In the bedrooms, seven beds stood neatly made up, with their white woolen blankets and their prim black coverlets. Outside the house, beached in a row as neatly as the beds, were the water craft, a fleet of dug-outs complete with oars and fishing tackle ready for use. From Pringle's description emerges the background of a life of comfort and modest charm in the wilderness, but with no hint of a former Norwood mansion built of stone.

Whether it was by chance or choice, or vague memories of his childhood stone mansion in England that persuaded Francis Norwood to settle on the granite hills and ledges of Cape Ann is not known. In any case, the stone abounding in the region was to play an important role in the unfolding drama of the Norwood legacy.

Meanwhile, a portion of Cape Ann's history had already been written. Old records presented a picture of an earlier Cape Ann, before the Norwoods and the Allens had received their grants and built their houses, a time when other Englishmen had sailed by their coast to take a look.

As early as 1605, Champlain had explored the Straitsmouth region, and another decade had brought the adventurer, John Smith, who wrote a blissful description of the area; "the paradise of all those parts that I have

Figure 11. Sandy Bay shoreline looking South

seen, could I but have means to transport a colony, I would rather live here than anywhere." John Smith came to Cape Ann in March 1614 and gave the region the name New England. "I have drawn a map," he said, "from point to point, with soundings, sands, rocks, and landmarks, as I passed close to shore in a small boat." Smith presented this map to King Charles I who approved the name for New England. He also agreed to Smith's choice of the romantic Tragabigzanda as a name for the new Cape but then, with a King's prerogative, changed his mind and named it Cape Ann in honor of his mother, the Queen. When Smith returned home to England he published a guidebook of his travels in the new England. Two years later, he spent a summer in Cornwall and Devonshire, distributing copies to the nobility in these maritime counties. Already the guidebook's Cape Ann was being called "The Paradise of New England."

By the time Cape Ann received her charter in 1645, fishermen were beginning to come and settle. But even before the fishermen came, Pringle tells us, "Cape Ann was a thriving settlement of Red Men," who were already using the great quantities of fish, wood, water, and stone that John Smith had praised so highly.

Although now settled in a new land with his growing family, Francis Norwood continued to live by the motto inscribed on the Norwood Heraldic Coat of Arms in their customary negatives, "Never unready." By the time he died in 1709, at the age of 72, he had acquired 170 acres of Cape Ann land. In his will, he left to Elizabeth "the lower floor of the western half of the house with cellar," with the stipulation that the family provide for her welfare with "cattle, hens, Indian corn, pork, apples, cider, and a horse for riding." The will, written in long-hand in great detail, provides a clear picture of the family life and indicates a considerable fortune in "current money of New England." Not only did he provide for his sons and his wife, but he also considered the welfare of his daughters and a granddaughter, Elizabeth, whose father, Stephen, had been lost by drowning. In his carefully considered will, he also specifically mentions his oldest son, Thomas. "I give and bequeath to my eldest son, Thomas Norwood, that I have formerly given him in money and other pay two shillings in money and all my wearing clothes that I leave behind me with my decease, both linen and woolen and what else of use to wear of all sorts. The reason that I give my son Thomas no more in this my will is because he went from me to his grandfather Clement Coldam when he was about the age of twelve, and upon that account he was settled in the house and lands in the township of Lin, an instrument being in my hand and seal never to trouble nor disturb my executors after my decease for any more of my estate but what I was pleased to bestow on him in this my last Will and Testament."

As the Norwoods claimed their land grants at Cape Ann, the craggy shoreline became increasingly important to them. They soon learned that the areas of dense woods disguised acres of rocky soil. Sixteen miles of waterfront zigzagged around the Sandy Bay section of Cape Ann, Gloucester's fifth parish, —"rugged and rockbound," one said, "but with good sandy beaches." Another historian, John White Marshall, described in greater detail the surface of the town as "hill and dale, with bold, precipitous ledges of rock, and acres of boulders of all sizes, from many tons weight to water pail size, while fruit trees and acres of woods grew in abundance."

The Norwoods adapted to their new surroundings, making good use of land, water, and stone, while learning from the "Red Men" the skills required for such use. But in Gloucester, knowledge of the "Red Men" was not widespread until the year 1700, when Samuel English, asserting to be the grandson of Chief Masconomet, emerged as leader of the native Indians, and demanded payment for the land now settled on by white men and named by them Cape Ann.

Joseph Allen, forty-six years old, and forty-one-year-old William

Figure 12. Sandy Bay shoreline looking North

Stevens, an officer in the militia, were chosen to meet and negotiate with the Red Men. Some twenty-five years earlier the Allen family had settled on the south side of the Cape. A blacksmith by trade, with seventeen children, Joseph was now a selectman, had served the town in other official positions, had begun to acquire more land, and was a leading citizen. For many generations his descendants were to become influential citizens of Gloucester. One early writer described the Allen family as "having marked ability, and a family of culture who held a high social position in Gloucester." Joseph Allen and William Stevens set the date of December 25, 1700, to meet and discuss ownership of Cape Ann. Nature intervened, however, with a raging snowstorm, so furious that they were forced to postpone the meeting. When they finally met, on January 14, 1701, they agreed to a fair exchange of 10,000 acres, although the deed was not enacted until July 1, six months later to the day. This delay was due to the fact that no money had yet been raised "to pay for the Township of Samuel English Indian." Samuel English, unable to read the agreement, or to sign his name, made it official with his personal mark, looking somewhat like a capital C with a capital A resting on the top. Cape Ann paid seven British pounds for its 10,000 acres of forest and pasture land, an amount equal to $1000 in today's market. Gloucester financed the purchase by selling off some of the lots held in common by the town. All Gloucester land titles date from this original deed.

By this time the total number of settlers had increased from 82 to 500 living at Cape Ann, who became active in fishing and trading. Some of the grants that Francis Norwood had received from the town, or had been able to buy, stretched south and east of Goose Cove toward that section of Gloucester known as Pigeon Cove. Although the Norwoods and other landowners had cleared many acres of land for building their homes, Pigeon Cove was still dense forest as late as 1670, and town officials already recognized the importance of restricted cutting in this pristine forest growth. Landowners had begun to suspect that unknown woodcutters were pilfering the valuable trees on their land without permission. But for various reasons, interest in forest conservation waned in favor of further development along the shore, one reason being that many of these lots had already been cleared, and fishing had become more important to them.

In 1707, a road was laid out from Goose Cove to Pigeon Cove, with gates erected for travelers to pass through farms that were privately owned. The land that Francis and Elizabeth had cleared for their house at Goose Cove followed this rough trail along the coast, easterly toward the land of Joshua, their fifth child and second son. Joshua had married another Elizabeth (Andrews) at the age of twenty-one, after working as crew on boats for five years. From his father's will Joshua received a gift of sixty acres of Pigeon Cove wilderness, on which he and Elizabeth were already settled. Although living surrounded by acres of remote woodland, Joshua and Elizabeth adjusted, nevertheless, to their Cape Ann environment. After crossing the Annisquam River they had found coves, inlets, and beaches beyond the trees, and had discovered the many craggy points jutting into the sea. Between the forest and the sea were stretches of alder, willows, barberry bushes, blueberries, fragrant bayberries, with wild pink roses clinging to massive granite boulders.

In 1704, Joshua's land, with other owners interspersed, began at the corner fence at the north end of what is now Curtis Street, and it covered the area where Joshua had already established his own home, first known as

Figure 13. The Garrison House also known as the Witch House Pigeon Cove

the "Garrison House" and later on as the "Witch House." The age of the old house is unclear, but 1688 is the earliest recorded date for a center portion made of logs. According to its late owner, Nadia Williams, the original section of this rambling structure was built by woodsmen sometime before that date, possibly as a refuge from Indians. It may have been identified as "The Garrison" when used as protection from assaults during King Phillip's War of 1675-76. Much later, by 1740, even with numerous changes and additions, it began to be called "The Old House." Nadia Williams estimated that the first section, a garrison-shaped building with a garret, was probably constructed about 1667-1675.‡ It is built of squared logs with a fortress overhang, and hewn by hand with an axe, displaying a craftsmanship so remarkable and so perfectly flat, that no space is visible between the logs, and not so much as a splinter can be felt when running a hand along the surface. Only a few small axe marks reveal that the logs were hand hewn. Finishing wood in this manner is a lost art today when few craftsmen have the skill to use an axe with such precision.

Another remarkable feature in the old house is a central walk-in fireplace, with its original log lintel still in place. The lintel extends an impressive eight feet across the entire fireplace. The ceiling is likewise supported by enormous beams that measure eighteen inches in width. The beams are a mere six feet above the floor, and although they are hewn smooth to the touch, they are not designed for today's taller people. In time, new additions provided shingles for greater warmth and erected as it was, directly on ledge, a new brick chimney enclosed a "bee-hive" oven with a cast iron door and its own flue. The oven was an "up-to-date" design made for the convenience of the housewife to bake more than one loaf of bread at a time.

Outside the dwelling, near an ox barn then to be shared with cows, as well as for storage for hay and barley, Joshua built small sheds to shelter pigs and chickens, with a pond of fresh water nearby. A hill protected the house from icy north winds in winter, but, facing to the south and southeast, Joshua and Elizabeth enjoyed summer breezes and a spectacular view of the ocean and coves.

In this lonely spot, as isolated a region as any on Cape Ann, Joshua raised his family and restored parts of the old house, a house that had already written its own secret episode for a chapter of Cape Ann history.

The dramatic incident affiliated with the "Old House" continues to be told after 300 years. In 1690, the story goes, an accusation of witchcraft had condemned an innocent woman in Salem. With her husband executed, her two sons had somehow struggled through the wilderness trail to seek refuge for her in the Old House. Her life had been spared because she was pregnant, with the stipulation that she seclude herself from all contact with anyone living in the community. Her sons could have found no more secluded hiding place for her exile than the Old House in the Pigeon Cove wilderness. With the ending of the witch trials in Salem a few years later, the Old House, once called the Garrison House, now became known as the Witch House, and this name remains in general use on Cape Ann.

The Witch House still retains its thick walls, low ceilings, corner posts and crossbeams, and enormous chimneys in contrast to tiny window panes. The flowering vines, planted by Joshua and Elizabeth, still wind around the veranda and partially hide weather-stained woodwork.

Joshua Norwood's acres followed the road at the opposite corner of the fence near Curtis Street. This Norwood land extended from Gott Avenue all the way to Back Beach and beyond, to the Mill Brook at Front Beach of Sandy Bay (now Rockport). At various times, it measured as sixty acres to over one hundred acres. By 1719, four farms had been settled between Joshua's property and the stone (keystone) bridge. One or another of the Norwood family owned this land for about one hundred years. (Then it was transferred to the Babson family and became known as Babson Farms.)

Meanwhile, in 1732, a restless Joshua, having sold his "Garrison House" to Elias Davis, a prosperous shipping merchant in Gloucester, moved his family to Attleboro for a period of eight years. Enroute to Attleboro, undoubtedly traveling by boat, the family stopped in Cambridge. While in Cambridge, arrangements were made for Mary, one of their six daughters, then about sixteen years of age, to remain with the family of a professor at Harvard College. In time, Mary met and married Nathaniel Gamage and bore several children. As Historian Ebenezer Pool wrote, "In 1740 old Nathaniel left his wife and family for parts not named to his wife. Suspicions are," he concluded, "that Nathaniel may have left for England to look up his estate as he was said to have been a descendant of Thomas Gamage, Lord High Chancellor of the King, Keeper of the Great Seal or Scribe to the King." After Joshua's eight years in Attleboro, he moved back to Cambridge where he found temporary employment at a tavern owned by his brother, Caleb.

The reason for these moves is not quite clear but Pringle states, perhaps with ironic intent, that "the controlling motive which impels men to seek their fortunes in new fields, or unknown climes, is generally to better their condition."

In the case of Joshua Norwood, several possible reasons for his moves have emerged over the years. Records show that Attleboro was positioned on the Boston Post Road, (Route One) the major thoroughfare between Boston and the ports of Narragansett Bay only 10 miles to the west. Money could be made, Joshua knew, in the exchange of fish for sugar and molasses, both used for the making of rum, and in the trade of other commodities. It is tempting to speculate that Elias Davis, who had bought Joshua's Pigeon Cove house, and whose family had already made substantial profits at privateering, may have dispatched him to Attleboro in the interests of both families. Tavern keeping, too, was a profitable business along the New England coast for members of the Norwood family. Taverns were set up in any building available, then used for trading, for decision-making by town officials, and often for church services. At this time, in Attleboro, activity centered on a ten-mile-long waterway leading to the sea. Privateers, and pirates, too, were at work in Narragansett Bay and it is probable that Joshua was exploring his chances of adding to his income. As a tavern keeper on the only highway, Joshua could have been a valuable agent and informant to the Davis family interests.

Whatever the reason for moving, Joshua and Elizabeth returned to Cape Ann about 1738, divided their Pigeon Cove acres among their children, having sold the Witch House to Elias Davis before they went to Attleboro. The two men were closely related in their families and in business ventures, and Elias, at age thirty-six, may have influenced Joshua in the move to Attleboro. The Davis family, with a history of ship owners and merchants, had already made substantial profit in privateering. When Elias died, two years after buying the Witch House, his holdings in addition to the Witch House included a house lot and wharf, a house and three acres of land at Sawmill Brook, yet another house and land, several schooners, and a fleet of dug-outs. This property was worth 5339 pounds. In a later appraisal of Joshua's holdings, his estate was valued at 4500 pounds and by comparison was said to be the second largest estate in Gloucester. Over many years thereafter, the Witch House changed hands ten times. First sold to Elias Davis, it went from the Davis family to John Proctor, then to Moses Wheeler, who had married one of Joshua's daughters. In 1848, the house passed to Elijah Edmunds, who had also married into the family. Four years later, Edmunds sold to his son, James, who re-sold it immediately to James Higginson. In another two years it was sold yet again to Joseph Babson, then to Hooker Coggeshall, and finally, in 1925, it went to its present owner, the Oliver Williams family. The house is now a private residence and is not open to the public.

‡The Witch House is presently undergoing a dendrochronology study, a precise scientific survey of its timbers to determine the year of construction. This is the science of tree-ring dating now used around the world to date historic material. Oak is the required wood for this study because of its strength and durability, but scientists often come upon beams of the tamarac, a tree almost as desirable, and sometimes preferred over the oak to use for house beams.

The wood in an old house such as the Witch House can be dated by taking core borings five-eighths of an inch in diameter from timbers that have been determined to have sufficient tree rings for study. The samples are small and are usually taken from an attic or some other out-of-sight location. The Witch House was found to have very little oak but more of the tamarac. This tree is also called hackmatack, a name coming from the aboriginal Algonquins and still in use in northern New England. It is also known as the larch, a general term used to determine strong conifers. The study is on-going and the SBHS hopes to have an exact dating for construction of the Witch House at a later date.

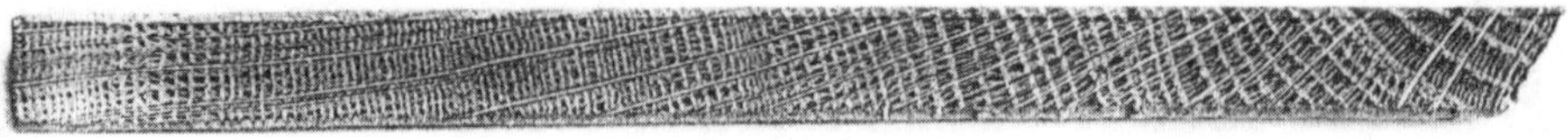

Example of tree core.

•••

STRAITSMOUTH • MOORING STONES • PRIVATEERS

•••

After selling his Pigeon Cove house, Joshua purchased more land across Sandy Bay, behind Straitsmouth Island, and added it to land he already owned there at Gap Head. Upon his return from Attleboro he then took over the land and a log house that he had purchased from John Babson. Log cabins of that day were built in the simplest of styles, with one window, and a single door always facing toward the south. The framework or design of this log cabin was said to have been brought from England. The one-room structures, though dimly lit, often sheltered large families. Within a few years, Joshua and Joshua, Jr. claimed their land grants at Straitsmouth, along with Francis (another son of Joshua), as well as with Joseph Allen.

The point of land called Straitsmouth, behind Straitsmouth Island, had been settled by a few landowners a decade earlier, and some "nomadic Pilgrims" who traveled north even earlier to explore the fishing potential. With forest and rocky pasture blending into the background, and surf of the Atlantic Ocean billowing toward their front door, the settlers fished for cod. In their small boats they fished from Ipswich on the north shore, all the way to Cape Cod on the south shore. After their long days of fishing, they landed their boatloads of fish at Straitsmouth Cove, where they then split them, removed the backbone, and prepared them to be salted, soaked, and placed on frames, to dry in the open air. Finally, they were shipped to the Caribbean or to home ports in Olde England. (See Plate A)

Over time, the elder Francis and Elizabeth acquired 180 Cape Ann acres, divided them among their ten children, and Joshua and his father became respected land owners, both men earning the distinguished title of

Figure 14. An ancient mooring stone removed from Old Harbor with the remains of an oak stump.

"Gentleman." The Norwood dynasty was underway on Cape Ann, and soon to be carried on by sons and daughters of Francis and Elizabeth.

Joshua, a man of many skills, had barely arrived at Straismouth to live among the fishermen, when he began to make mooring stones, a new industry just being established to accommodate the increasing number of fishing vessels. The fishermen-landowners now living there were already set up to make the mooring stones, and Joshua is credited as the first man, along with his son, Joshua, Jr., to cut the now historic round stone for the fishermen, a forerunner of the important industry of quarrying Cape Ann granite. These mooring stones were enormous slabs of granite sliced laboriously by hand from pieces of flat ledge that made up the foundation of Cape Ann. Each slab was cut six feet square, ten to fifteen inches thick, with a hole fifteen inches in diameter chiseled out of the center. Into this hole fishermen inserted the entire trunk of an oak tree, chosen for its special size, often as much as twenty feet long, with sections of the root still attached. These stones, weighing about two tons, were usually maneuvered onto a skid, with the aid of oxen, and then hauled to the waterfront. Here they were slipped onto a raft and poled to a point in Long Cove that the fisherman had chosen to moor his boat.

Life at Cape Ann was difficult for Joshua and others living at Straitsmouth in the mid-seventeen hundreds, and they all joined in the fishing, farming, and the making of mooring stones to support parents and sib-

Figure 15. Two mooring stones in the North Basin.

lings of their large families. Years later, when Joshua died, he had only land to leave to his heirs, but for a family that descended from near nobility, they were never "idle gentry." While the Norwood family acquired acres of land, they also earned a reputation for being hard workers.

The harsh, rough labor of fishing and the making of mooring stones was not the only challenge for the stone workers. The main street of Gloucester was still only a footpath, and lots were being granted to young men who were willing to build on them. Sandy Bay, Gloucester's fifth parish, was growing. With the steady increase in fishing and trade activity at Gully Cove, behind Straitsmouth Island, smuggling of commodities such as rum, sugar, and molasses became a common practice for pirates spying and scouting the coves of Cape Ann. The Norwood, Allen, and Davis families, along with their neighbors, haunted by the approach of these unwelcome visitors, and constantly on the alert for suspicious movements, were often tolerant, nevertheless, as many were British buccaneers from their homeland. These pirates, known as buccaneers, are said to be the first to use the term "barbecue" for their outdoor cooking. They first slaughtered and then smoked the meat of wild cattle on trestles, that they called "boucans," and from this British word evolved the word buccaneer.

As Massachusetts settlers neared their declaration of freedom from England, they were often unable to distinguish pirate ships lurking in their coves from vessels sailing as privateers with authorization from the

Continental Congress. The privateers were legalized for both profit and protection. They were private ships, fitted out at private expense, mainly to capture British or other ships suspected to be carrying war supplies. Government authorities granted two kinds of permits. One allowed the use of privately-owned vessels only as a privateer or ship of war. A second authorization was granted as a Letter of Marque allowing the ship to carry on trade, but also to have authority to capture foreign cargo. For years most merchant ships, especially those trading in the West Indies, had been fitted out with armament of some kind to protect themselves. Manning the vessels with crews adapted to the sea became a natural pursuit for Gloucester mariners, though the risks were great and often required many months of absence at sea without profits from enemy vessels or cargoes.

As early as 1717, local fishermen had feared their waters were being over-run by pirates who were ready to capture their cargo or their ships. Not all pirate ships, as some believed, searched for gold or other treasures. To many of that time, wood and water were equally desirable to them, and these they found in plentiful supply along the New England coast. In April 1724, one pirate ship had captured several vessels off Cape Cod and had succeeded in taking two Gloucester fishermen as captives. Since this incident more seizures had taken place, sometimes with cargoes of salt taken, but often a cargo of fish was taken and re-sold for a high price.

In the spring of 1724, the first known confrontation with pirates in local waters occurred at Goose Cove, in full sight of the Francis Norwood house. Construction of a new vessel, *The Squirrel*, was all but finished and the crew preparing for its trial run, when a pirate gang, long feared for their frequent harassment of Gloucester ships, boarded in stealth and commanded the crew to complete the carpentry under guard. The owners, however, resolved not to give up to a pirate seizure, at least without a struggle to hold their new ship. To recapture their vessel, they devised a courageous plan to await a signal at noon, when the pirates might be momentarily idle and off guard, and then, with their carpenters' tools, overpower their captors and take back their ship. Not only did the bold plan succeed, historians recorded, but Captain Andrew Harraden sailed *The Squirrel* back into Goose Cove, with the head of John Phillips swinging from the mast. John Nott, a pirate almost as notorious and feared as the well-known Captain Kidd, was hanged from a tree on a nearby island. Captain Kidd, incidentally, was forty-two

Figure 16. Aerial scene of (from left to right) Straitsmouth Cove, Gap Cove, Gap Head, Straitsmouth Island, Gully Point Cove and Gully Point

years old in 1696. He had made his way from his home in Scotland to the Caribbean, and eventually up the coast of New England, where he was put behind bars in Boston in 1699, and posed no threat at this time to Cape Ann fishermen.

For arrests of this kind, justice was usually swift. In Gloucester, with the capture of *The Squirrel*, one pirate victim was tossed overboard, some were beheaded with any weapon at hand on the new vessel, and still others were hanged on a tree on "Hangman's Isle." A few were reprieved "to the King's mercy." Fear of further encounters, along with rumors of pirates seeking shelter in their many hidden coves and inlets, raised constant alarm among the Cape Ann settlers at Straitsmouth.

The years 1713 to 1776 were considered the "heyday" of trading that was in violation of the law. Joshua Norwood, when in his eighties, was said to have made a habit of watching the pirates whenever they came ashore near Straitsmouth, usually at night, noting their activities and stealthy movements. Sometimes Cape Ann mariners, too, were as merciless as the pirates in finding ways to make a profit.

During the American Revolution, fourteen Gloucester vessels participated in such stealthy maneuvers, though some in Gloucester felt it was contrary to their ethics. Pirate crews not always known to Cape Ann, however, were less concerned about their ethical standards. It was rumored that some would pretend to be lighthouses and trick ships into crashing against the rocks, and then row out to scavenge the cargo. The pirates who scouted the Cape Ann shoreline were said to have their own secret harbors, with Gully Point and Gap Cove, behind Straitsmouth Island, among their favorites.

Figure 17. 'Digging for Gold,' original illustration by H. Boyslton Dummer for the book: *Alluring Rockport: an Unspoiled New England Town on Cape Ann*

•••

THE YEAR 1771 • CALEB'S GOLD •

•••

Caleb, the youngest son of Joshua and Elizabeth, was two years old when the family moved back from Attleboro to Straitsmouth on Cape Ann. He spent his boyhood growing up at Straitsmouth. By the time he was ten years old, Caleb had learned how to fish off the rocks and from a small boat. He talked in terms the fishermen used, and every style of boat and sail were familiar sights to him. His father taught him how to clear the gravelly surface of rocks and pebbles, and how to plant seed in order to vary the family's diet of codfish and other food from the ocean. He knew his neighbors and worked with them as brothers. Caleb knew that a "gundalow" was a broad raft or scow with a small sail, designed to collect a harvest of salt hay to fertilize their meager soil. So rocky the soil, and so close to the shore were they, that even their farms depended upon harvest of the sea.

Caleb, nicknamed "Red Cap" because of the red military cap that he wore as an act of defiance against the British, and his brother, Joshua, Jr., continued to live at Straitsmouth, near Gap Cove. At the age of twenty-four, Caleb married another Elizabeth (Grover) but after ten years of marriage and bearing five children, Elizabeth died. Caleb was left with the care of five young children and he lost no time in finding another wife in Ipswich. Within three months, Caleb married (1770) Jerusha Story. Two more children were soon added to the family; Francis (known as "Major"), born in 1771, and William, born three years later.

The year Francis was born, 1771, is a date to be etched into Cape Ann history, not merely because of the birth of this third generation Francis, but because of other notable events that occurred that year at Cape Ann.

Figure 18. View taken on Thacher Island of North and South Towers, Keepers House, and Whistle House .

First there were activities on Thacher Island, a large island two miles off-shore from Straitsmouth, and a landmark familiar to all mariners who sailed the New England coast. After the Thacher shipwreck that occurred in 1636, the Massachusetts General Court at Salem presented the island to Anthony Thacher and his wife who were the only survivors of this tragedy. Even though they never lived there, the island remained in the Thacher family for eighty years, when Thacher heirs sold it to the Reverend John White. John White owned the island for ten years to use as pasturage for his oxen, but found he could make a profit by selling it to the prosperous Gloucester merchant, Joseph Allen. Joseph Allen and his family kept the island to pasture their own oxen until 1771. In that memorable year of 1771, Allen heirs sold the island to three Gloucester men, who in turn sold it to a committee of six men who were authorized by the Massachusetts Bay Colony to buy the island and erect a lighthouse there. The importance of the lighthouse to merchants and mariners of Cape Ann was now publicly recognized for the first time.

But in this same eventful year of illuminating the lighthouses on Thacher Island, a second momentous event occurred, an event so hard to believe that visitors, as well as native Cape Anners, have debated its accuracy for generations. For this was the year that rumors began to spread that Caleb Norwood had discovered a cache of pirate gold.

For over two hundred years many variations of Caleb's discovery have been told and re-told, and for all those years the doubts have lingered to tantalize believers and skeptics, while endless arguments failed to settle the

Figure 19. View of Gully Point from the site of the Norwood cabin

doubts. Opinions ranged from complete disbelief to absolute verification of the value of Caleb's find. But researchers Donald Dawson and Peter Bergholtz have now put together persuasive evidence of the existence of Caleb Norwood's treasure.

One of the earliest written records of this incredible and exciting event came to light in Historian Ebenezer Pool's papers at the Sandy Bay Historical Library. Historian Pool wrote in his diary that "the money find was not made public, but was of many thousands value," and his report concluded that it was found "south of the seashore Gully, near the cart rut as yet used."

As the years went on, with many variations of the stories narrated, it was at first believed that Caleb was a boy of thirteen, working one day in the nearby field of Francis Pool at Gully Point. On the contrary, further research revealed that Caleb, born in 1736, was a man of thirty-five in 1771, who was believed to have unearthed a container of gold "ingots"—that is, pieces in the form of gold bars—at the south end of Gully Cove, a familiar and favorite hide-out for pirates. While certain definitive items of proof could not be found, other records not only provided further assurance of Caleb's discovery, but also affirmed that he shared his find with his neighbor, Francis Pool, who owned the land on which the pieces of gold were believed to have been found.

As reassurance for the many skeptics, another piece of evidence came to light among the papers of historian John White Marshall, now preserved in the archives of the SBHS. Historian Marshall described the find as "uncoined gold (meaning without stamp or authority of the government) in one ounce pieces." In later years he re-stated, "We have good reason to believe that Caleb Norwood found buried, near the South Gully at Gully Point, from 7000 to 10,000 pounds (British currency) in gold." (Note: Historian Marshall was in a position to know of the gold first hand as he and Caleb's son, Caleb Jr., at one time, shared in the first Sandy Bay fish business, established in 1837.) This amount, our researchers found, converts to an amount somewhere between $490,000 to $700,000 in today's values. In these conversions of currency, it is necessary to take into account that there was no index for guidance and therefore some inaccuracies occurred over the long period of time. Furthermore, conversion rates between dollars and British pounds sterling varied widely from month to month and from region to region. Dollars were not in general use here until the Revolutionary War, and pounds were still in use until the 1790s. John Adams wrote in his diary, when enroute to Salem by ferry, that he saw "five boxes of dollars containing about eighteen thousand of them, going in a horse cart to Salem Custom House and to Boston, in order to be shipped to England."

With all the uncertainty in the monetary system, there was much guesswork in values but a conservative estimate of Caleb's 10,000 pounds in 1771 gives a conversion value of $700,000 in the recent year of 2001. In addition, state records of Massachusetts indicate that, in 1775, four years after his find, many citizens loaned funds to help finance the American Revolution. At this time, it was noted, the treasurer accepted such funds and paid interest on bonds at a rate of six percent ($1.10 per day) until redeemed by the state. This indicates that Caleb had made such loans to the state treasury. Most of this money, incidentally, went into the buying of guns and supplies, stipends for war widows, and for "paying the rolls" of the soldiers, many from their own Essex County, who were fighting the battles of the Revolution. The accounts, consistent in every detail with investments made by Cape Ann men, revealed in the same ledger payments made to Paul Revere and John Adams, as well as reimbursements for entertaining George Washington. According to these records, citizens were paid for guns and other supplies left behind after the Battle of Bunker Hill, a conflict in which sixty-six Cape Ann men participated.

The Massachusetts archives, at Columbia Point in Boston, contain

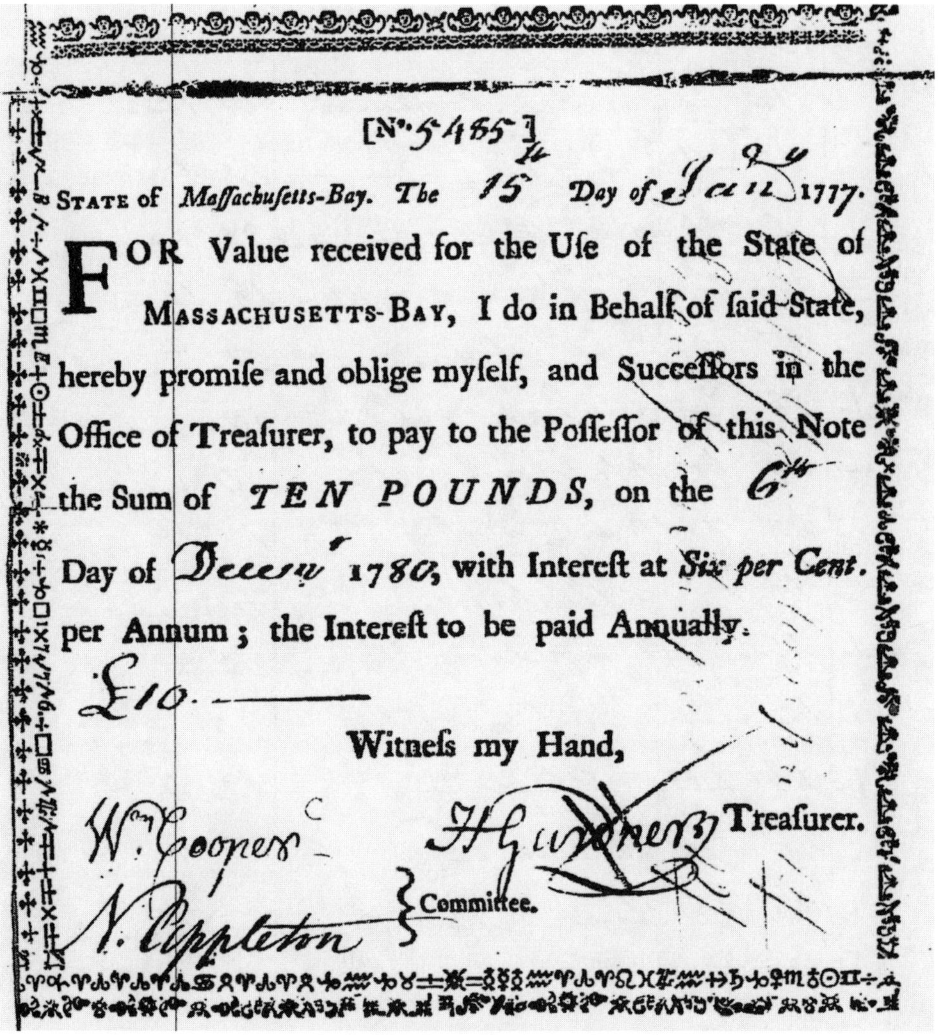

[N°. 5485]

STATE of *Massachusetts-Bay.* The 15 Day of Jan. 1777.

FOR Value received for the Use of the State of MASSACHUSETTS-BAY, I do in Behalf of said State, hereby promise and oblige myself, and Successors in the Office of Treasurer, to pay to the Possessor of this Note the Sum of *TEN POUNDS*, on the 6th Day of Decem.r 1780, with Interest at *Six per Cent.* per Annum; the Interest to be paid Annually.

£10. ——

Witness my Hand,

H Gardner Treasurer.

W.m Cooper
N. Appleton } Committee.

Figure 20. An example of a 6 % Bond issued by the new State of Massachusetts Bay to help finance the Revolutionary War

many of these oldest records of America's beginnings, and they have recently been re-organized by an archivist and made available to researchers. The ledgers contain state financial transactions of the Revolutionary War period. While some ledgers were missing in the state archives for those years, and Caleb Norwood's name could not be found in the exact years, one ledger disclosed a memo that "Notes were issued for Gold and Silver in 1777." The name of Francis Pool was listed as one who had received an interest payment of 45 pounds 8 shillings, in 1777, for gold that he had put into the bond pro-

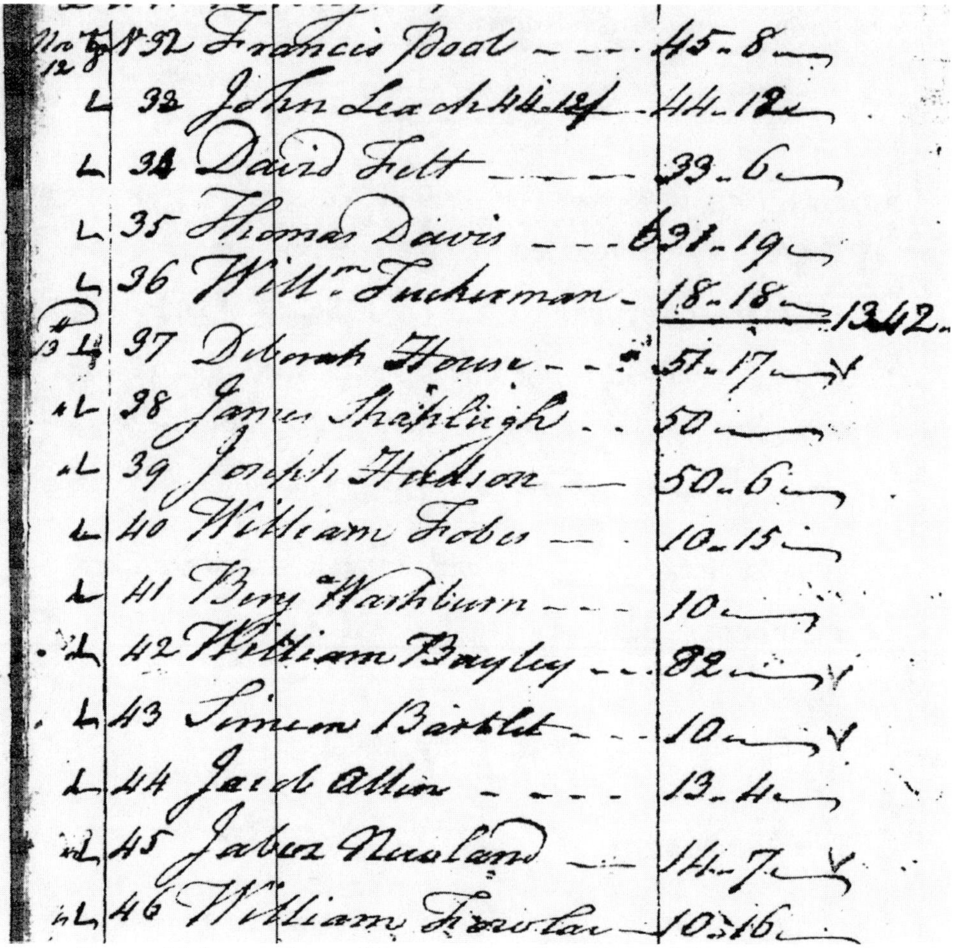

No 32	Francis Pool	45-8
33	John Lex [illegible]	44-12
34	David Felt	39-6
35	Thomas Davis	31-19
36	Willm Tucker[illegible]	18-18
		1342
37	Deborah House	51-17
38	James Stathligh	50
39	Joseph [illegible]	50-6
40	William [illegible]	10-15
41	Benj Washburn	10
42	William Bayley	82
43	Simeon Bartlet	10
44	Jacob Allen	13-4
45	Jabez Newland	14-7
46	William [illegible]	10-16

Figure 21. A ledger page showing "Notes issued for gold and silver 1777" that lists Francis Pool

gram. The interest for this amount, at a rate of 6%, as received by Francis Pool, is equal to $3200 in today's dollars. The value of Francis Pool's total loan to the state, in today's dollars, would amount to approximately $53,000. At that time thousands of New Englanders were recorded as sending money to purchase the bonds.

According to the treasury records, the state raised over $4,000,000 dollars, in addition to taxes paid by towns such as Gloucester, to help pay for the Revolution. The name of Francis Pool is noted in a Norwood family business ledger, preserved in the archives of the SBHS. A cryptic entry of December 24, 1771, states "this day rekned with Mr. Francis Pool and balanced all accounts." While most of the entries are written in considerable

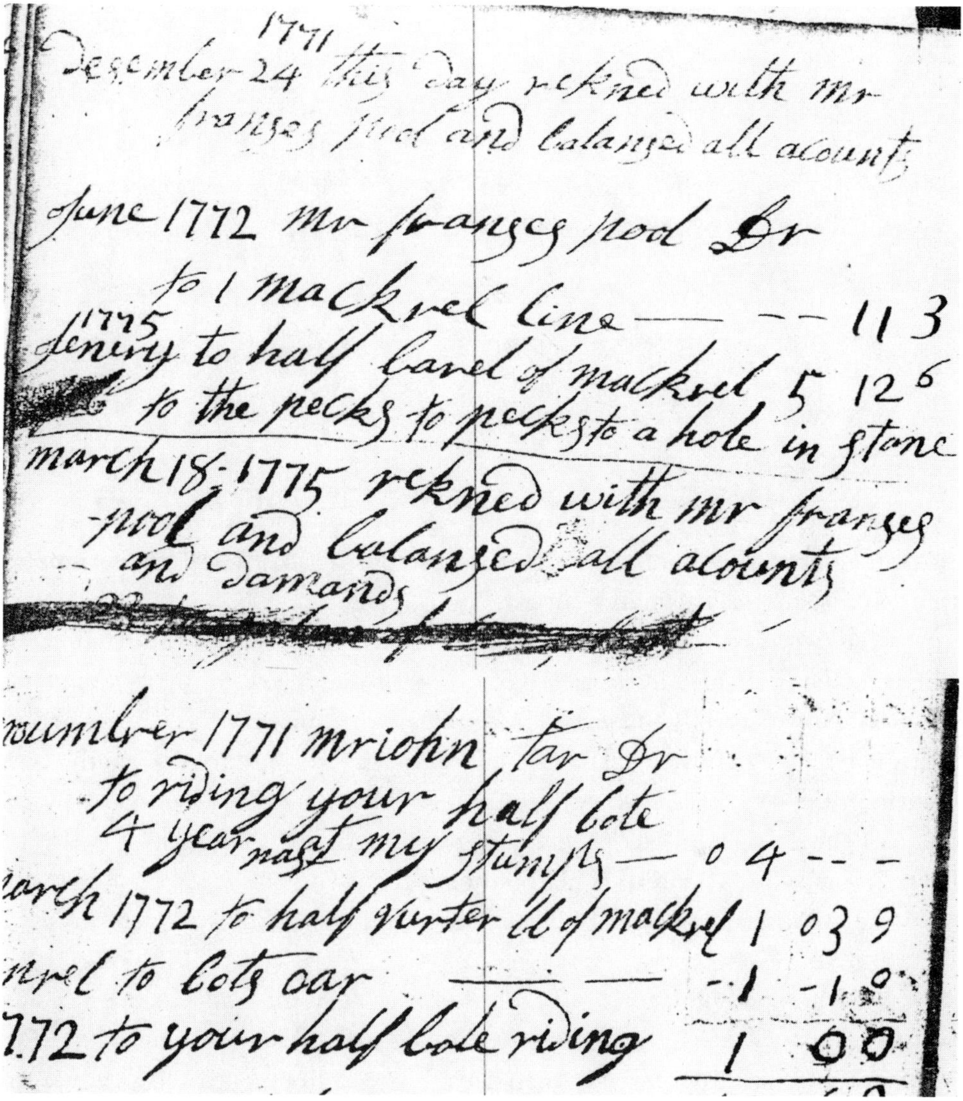
1771
december 24 this day rekned with mr
franses pool and balansed all acounts
June 1772 mr frances pool Dr
to 1 mackrel line —— -- 1 1 3
1775 Jenewry to half barel of mackrel 5 12 6
to the pecks to pecks to a hole in stone
march 18 1775 rekned with mr franses
pool and balansed all acounts
and damands
vember 1771 mr iohn tar Dr
to riding your half bote
4 year nast my stumps — 0 4 -- -
arch 1772 to half qurter ll of mackrel 1 0 3 9
rel to bots oar —— —— -1 -1 0
1772 to your half bote riding 1 0 0

Figure 22. A page from the Norwood family ledger showing an entry by Caleb Norwood that settled accounts with Francis Pool

detail, the brevity of the transaction about this reckoning led to further investigation. Along with the treasury records, they noted that Francis Pool was again "rekned with" on March 17, 1775. Two months later, on May 29, at the age of forty-four, he enlisted in John Rowe's Cape Ann Company, and in another month he had not only invested a fortune in the Revolution, he gave his life at the Battle of Bunker Hill. When his accounts were again settled

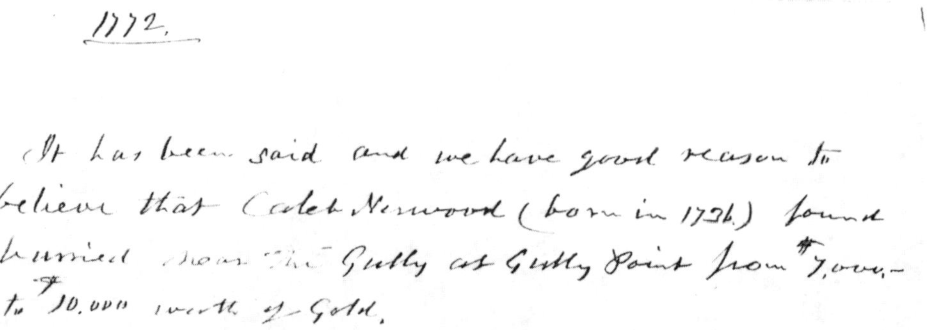

1772.

It has been said and we have good reason to believe that Caleb Norwood (born in 1736) found buried near the Gully at Gully Point from #7,000.- to #10,000 worth of Gold.

Figure 23. From the note of Jabez Tarr relating to the ingot gold found by Caleb Norwood

two years later, they indicated that interest on his loan to the government went to his son, also named Francis.

In addition to the assurance of both John White Marshall and Ebenezer Pool, a third authoritative source provided still more evidence of the gold. Now carefully preserved in the library of the SBHS is a note, handwritten by Jabez Tarr, a citizen then preparing to serve with Sandy Bay Militia in the War of the Revolution. Jabez Tarr states in his note: "I saw a piece of the gold in Ingot." (A mass of metal ready for shaping as noted earlier). At the same period of time, further records show that Caleb Norwood gave \$1000 dollars to each of his sons, Stephen and John, who were preparing to move to Maine.

Although Ebenezer Pool recorded that the find had not been made public, rumors of Caleb's fortune continued to spread into the next year when he purchased from the Allen family the sixteen acre plot known as Allen's Head. Then, at about the same time, he moved his log cabin from Straitsmouth to Long Cove, where new and larger boats were being moored.

The time had come for Don and Peter to review the accumulated evidence. Their own questions surfaced again and again. Although convinced themselves that the treasure had existed, were these pieces of evidence sufficient to convince the doubters? Had they overlooked any shred of proof in the library of the SBHS? Could there be as yet uncovered, more persuasive documentation to confirm their find?

Figure 24.[L] Joshua Norwood's cabin moved from Gap Head to Atlantic Ave
[R] Joshua Norwood's cabin at Atlantic Ave

They continued to debate other possibilities. With many privateers and pirates on the coast of Massachusetts during much of the 1700s, it was possible that Caleb, from the excellent vantage point of his log cabin window at Straitsmouth, could have observed any furtive movements at Gap or Straitsmouth Coves. The possibility could not be overlooked, also, although there was little evidence to substantiate the theory, that Caleb and his business associate, Francis Pool, were involved in some coastal privateering, and had somehow acquired the gold on their own. They were both experienced mariners, and both had long followed the sea with their fishing boats. Caleb now began to invest not only in more land, but he also moved to a larger house to replace his log cabin, when it would have been natural for his neighbors to wonder where the money came from for such purchases.

Figure 25. Aerial view of the harbor (Long Cove) with the Headlands at the lower left

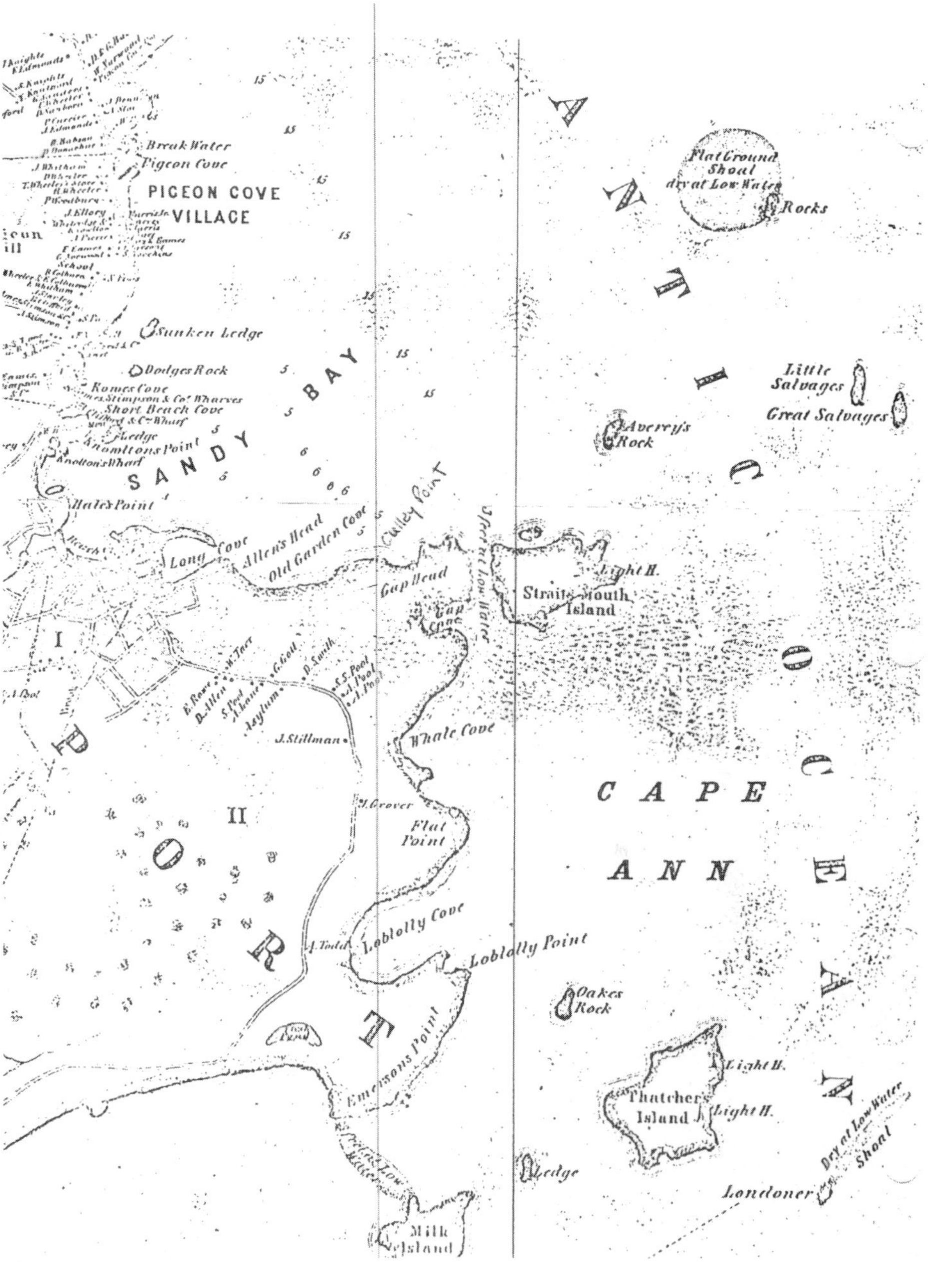

Walling Map of Cape Ann 1851

PLATE A

PRE-SETTLEMENT

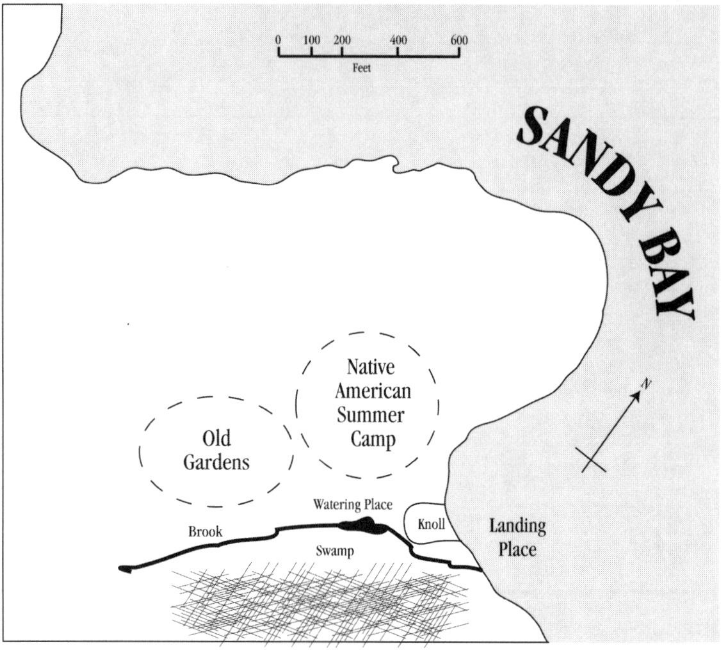

1708 - 1721 Grants to Commoners

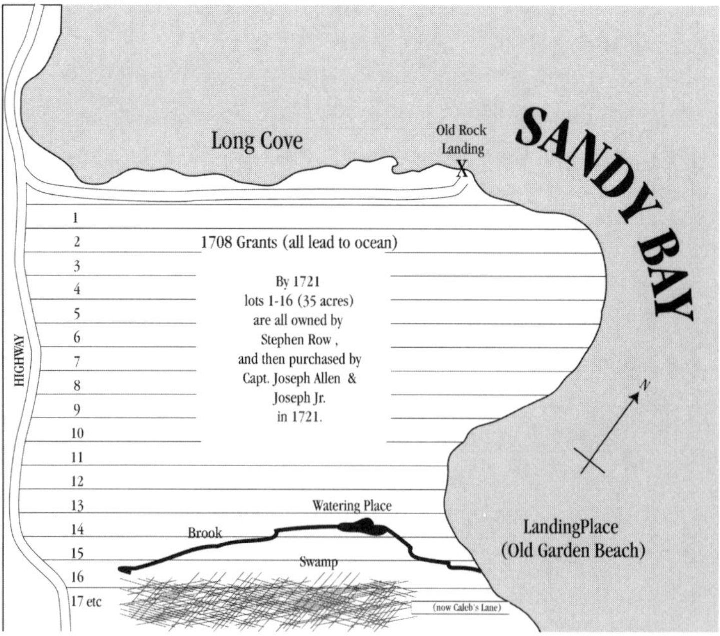

PLATE B

1721- 1772

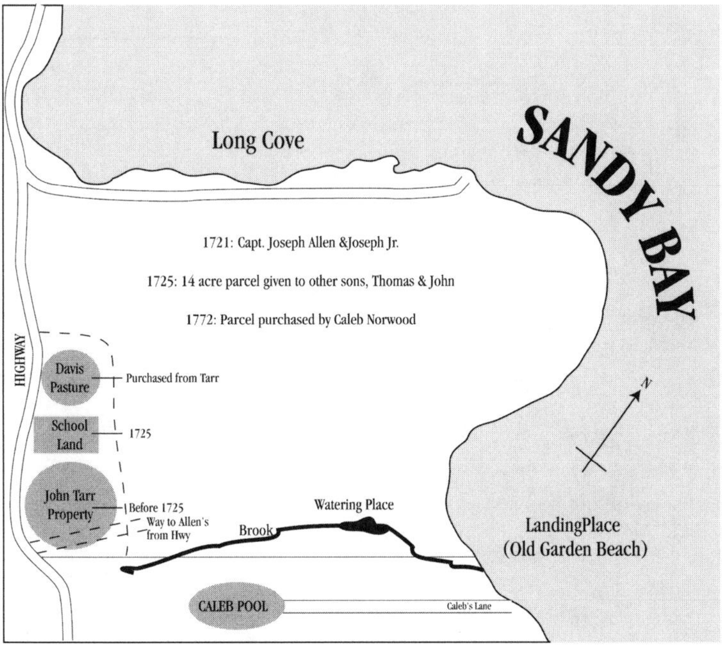

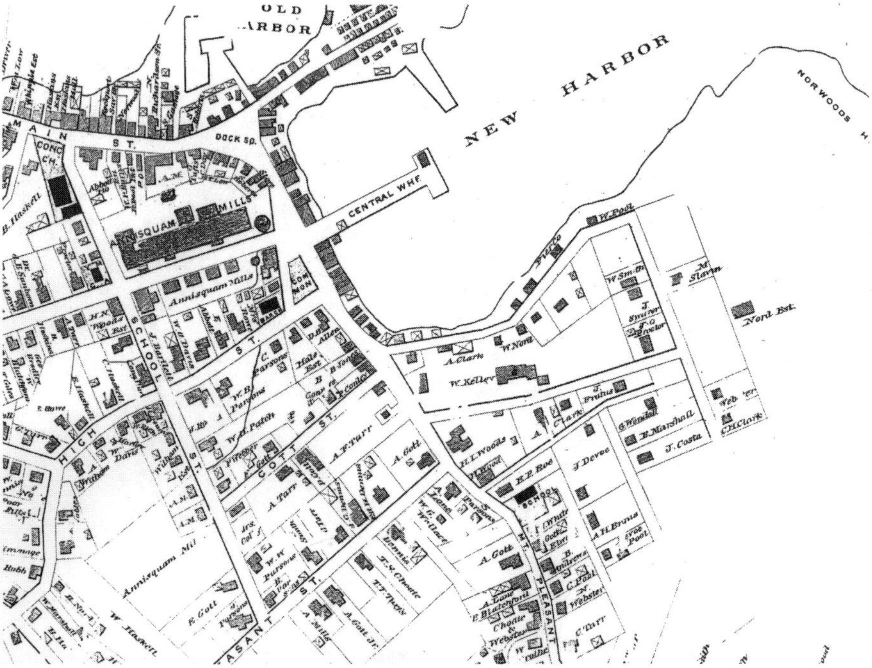

Norwood's Head

PLATE C

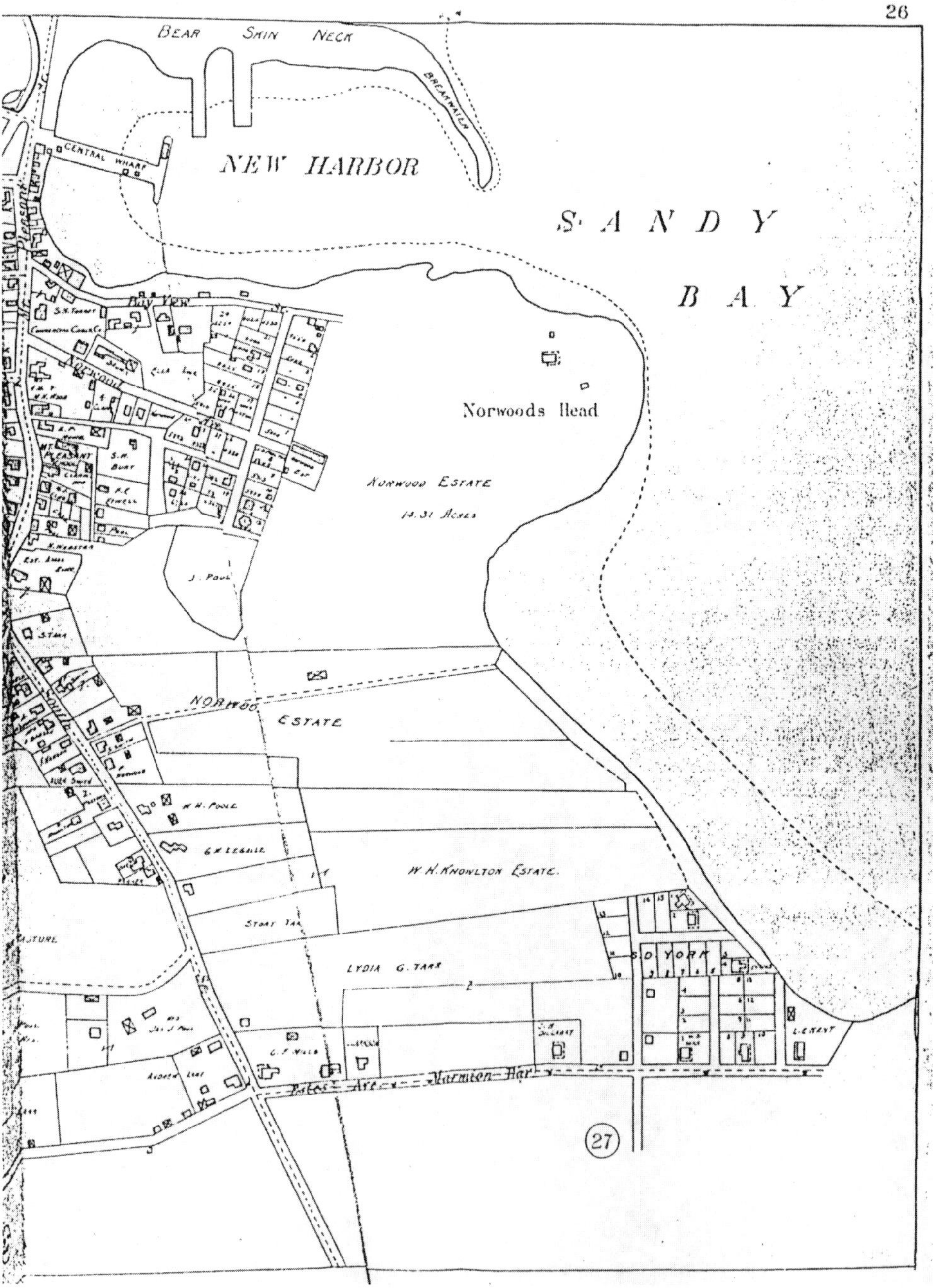

Norwood's Head (Courtesy of Louis F. Norwood, Jr.)

PLATE D

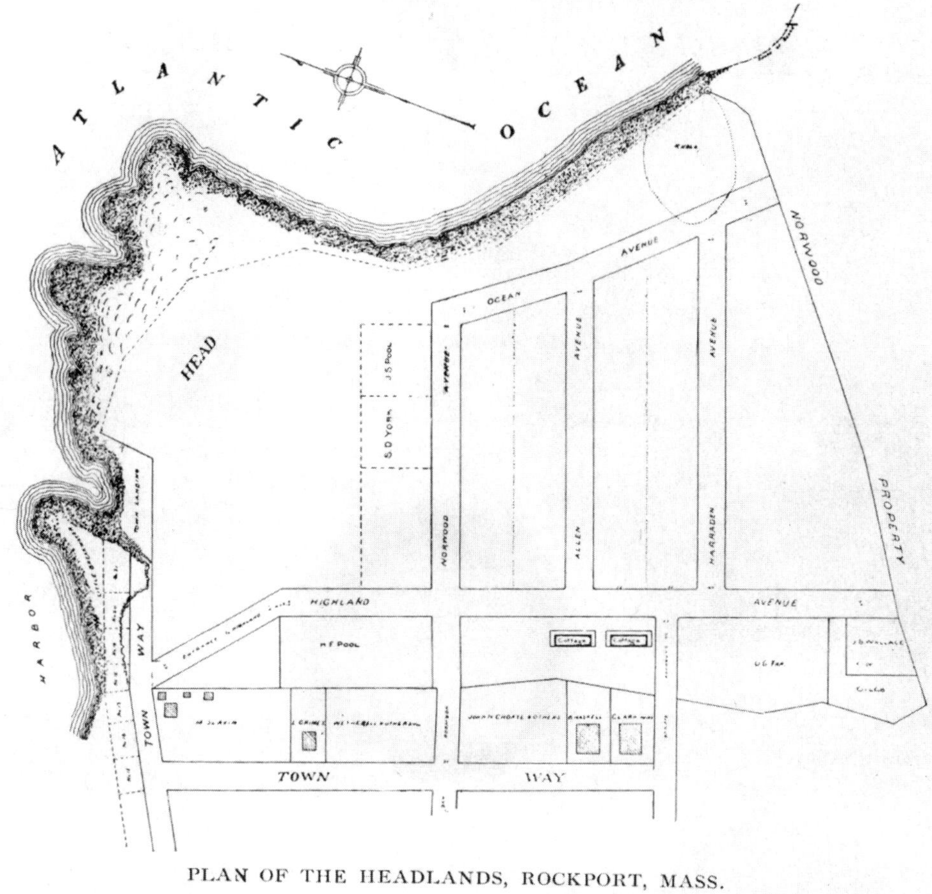

PLAN OF THE HEADLANDS, ROCKPORT, MASS.

PLATE E

NORWOOD HOUSES - SOUTH VILLAGE

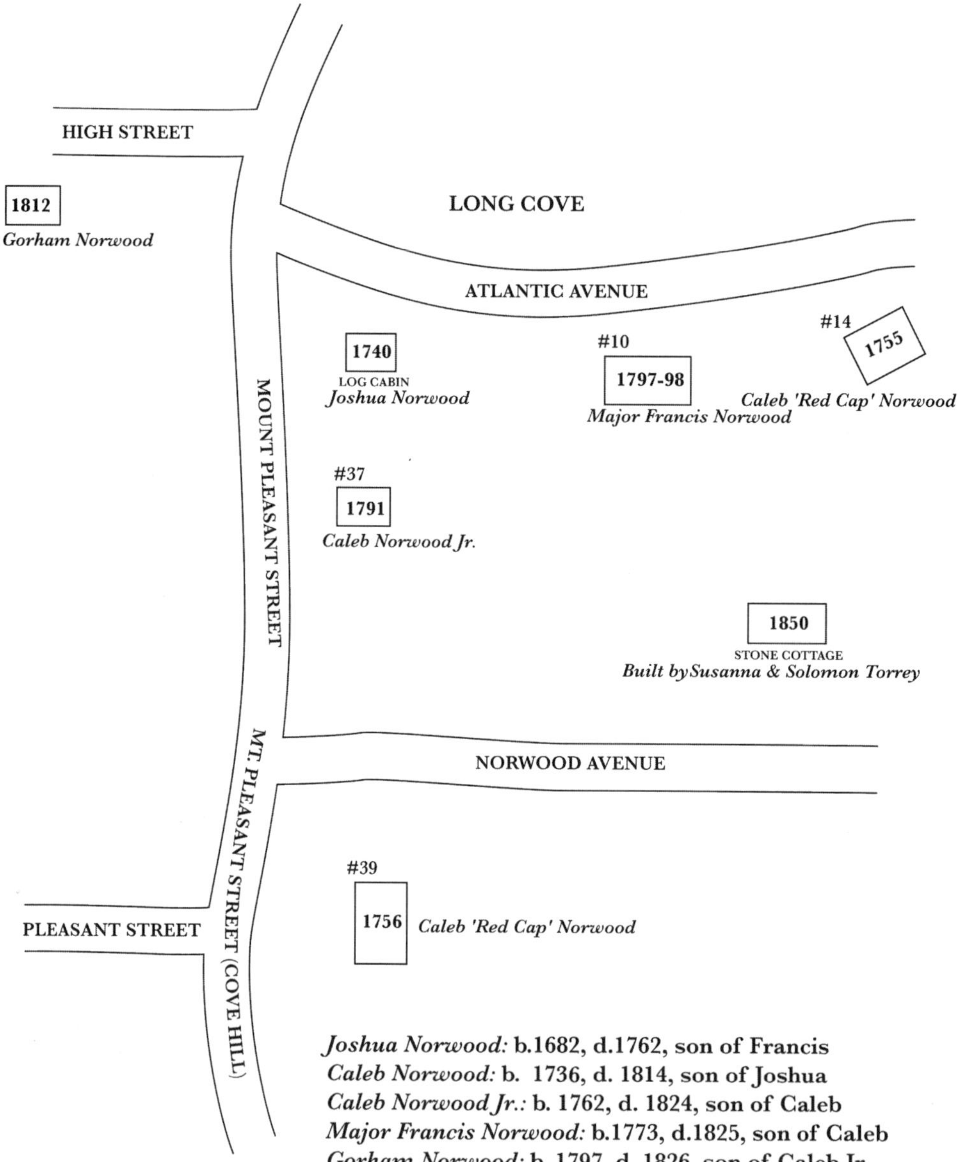

Joshua Norwood: **b.1682, d.1762, son of Francis**
Caleb Norwood: **b. 1736, d. 1814, son of Joshua**
Caleb Norwood Jr.: **b. 1762, d. 1824, son of Caleb**
Major Francis Norwood: **b.1773, d.1825, son of Caleb**
Gorham Norwood: **b. 1797, d. 1826, son of Caleb Jr.**

1998 Drawing by Cynthia A. Peckham, from a description in 'Norwood Notes' by C. Upham.

PLATE F

• • •

• HEADLANDS • ALLEN'S HEAD • NORWOOD'S HEAD

• • •

In 1772, the year following the report of Caleb's discovery of gold, Caleb moved his cabin, built in 1740, from Straitsmouth to the edge of Sandy Bay harbor. Whether he made the move around Allen's Head by water, or with oxen by way of the one mile cart road along the shore is not known. In any case, he placed his log house on his own land, at the corner of what is now Mt. Pleasant Street and Atlantic Avenue. Only a narrow path and a banking separated the cabin from new sailing vessels, and their mooring stones that his father, Joshua, had made. Within a few months of that same year, Caleb had proceeded to purchase "Allen's Head" from heirs of Joseph Allen, Jr.

Allen's Head was a tract of thirty-five acres, with Caleb's log house on one corner. Long Cove formed its northern boundary, with Sandy Bay and Old Garden Beach terminating its eastern limits. A southern boundary line then ran from the shore to the highway (Mt. Pleasant Street) near today's Caleb's Lane, then to the west and back to Long Cove.

The acreage that Caleb purchased in 1772 was part of a rocky point lying along the shore north of Straitsmouth, consisting of sixteen narrow lots originally assigned (in 1708) by lottery or purchase to sixteen commoners. (See Plate B) Called by John Smith "Ye Faire Headlands," and later known simply as "Ye Headlands," it was described as "hilly land and craggy shore." After the grants were assigned, one of the first owners, Stephen Row, bought the entire tract, but soon resold to Gloucester merchants Joseph Allen and his son, Joseph, Jr. for the price of 120 pounds. John Pool and his sons appear to have owned several grants, and it is possible that a portion of the original

Figure 26. View of Long Cove in the 1800's showing Pool's Fish Store and fishing boats at T Wharf

thirty-five acre parcel may have already been sold to John Tarr, but his ownership is not clear. Records show that a passageway had been established to run to the Allen property, through property owned by John Tarr. (From Mt. Pleasant Street to Burt Avenue, off Norwood Avenue.) Another piece of the parcel appears to have been purchased by the town of Gloucester to be used for a schoolhouse. The elder Joseph Allen, said to be the largest landowner of his time, died three years later at age 72, and his son inherited the property, naming it Allen's Head. (See Plate C)

Old records describe the Allen property as "running from the highway, on ye northwest side of ye lot to ye sea, thence running by ye sea to Long Cove, so called, to pitch pine marked '1', which belonged to Captain John Harraden; thence running on ye northwest side of ye first lott, to ye highway first mentioned." The deed goes on in its attempt to make clear the ownership, including "all ye land within ye said bounds, excepting ye lott which is owned by ye heirs of Jonathan Stevens, deceased, with all timber, wood, and trees, growing on ye land."

At this extreme end of Cape Ann, the property faced the ocean with a full view of the harbor and all the surrounding shoreline. In clear weather

Figure 27. Star Island with fish houses

even the Isle of Shoals was visible off the New Hampshire coast. The area was described as "bold" and "commanding," with the protection of Straitsmouth Island on its south side, and the entire harbor of Sandy Bay on its north shore. At the same time, it was known as mostly a brier-covered pasture, favored by wives of the fishermen for picking blueberries for their pies, bayberries for candle making, and for harvesting the crimson berries of alder bushes as autumn decorations. In the spring, windflowers and golden dogtooth violets blended with acres and acres of delicate pink mountain laurel.

Joseph Allen, Jr., having served as selectman and treasurer, still owned the property at his death in 1750. It then went to his daughter, Martha, and her husband, Aaron Smith of Marlboro, who held it for nearly twenty-five years. In this notable year, 1772, a Smith daughter, also named Martha, and married to a clergyman, Josiah Bridge of Sudbury, then inherited "35 acres more or less," apparently meaning the thirty-five acres minus the Tarr and schoolhouse lots. The Bridge family, at this time living "off the place" (an old Cape Ann expression for outsiders) and having little interest in their inheritance, sold Allen's Head to Caleb Norwood for "160 pounds lawful money."

The northeast shore of The Headlands tract, as noted, touched upon Long Cove where fishermen were beginning to anchor their boats. In another ten years, those living near the shore could count four fishing schooners and twenty-five smaller boats. In yet another decade Lucretia Norwood, known as "the old lady," counted sixty-two boats in Long Cove, most of them in view of the Norwood homes. The nearby lots, convenient for the fishermen, were drawn off in rectangular divisions that ran to the sea. The long, narrow shape for each lot was chosen deliberately to provide individual lot owners, as required by law, a free and open access to their moorings.

The Headlands remained in the holdings of Caleb Norwood for over forty years, meanwhile undergoing many divisions in order to accommodate the large Norwood family. When Caleb died, in 1814, at the age of seventy-eight, he left a fourteen-acre piece, nearest the shore, to his three sons, Caleb, Jr., William, and Francis. This tract, bounded by The Great Stone Wall, so impressive for its length and the size of its stones, was left in common as a pasture, and each son received two cow rights for a total of six cow rights in the parcel. By this time the area was named Norwood's Head. (See Plate D)

By the year 1854, the Norwood pasture, (still called by many Allen's Head) was chosen as the site of Rockport's Fourth of July celebration, the first in its history, and fourteen years after its separation from Gloucester. The area selected for setting up the tents belonged to William Norwood. When the committee in charge of events asked William for permission to use his pasture for the festivities he willingly agreed, and though the air was still a chilly April in Rockport, the committee got their elaborate July plans underway.

The day of the celebration at William Norwood's pasture, July 4, 1854, dawned hot and sultry. All arrangements were complete for the expected crowds and a long day of celebration. At sunrise, bells rang in the steeples and clanged at the cotton mill for a full half hour, and someone shot off a canon to greet the large number of guests already pouring into the town.

Bowers of flowers, flags, and bunting arched over the streets that led from the center of town to Norwood's Head. The parade formed on Broadway at 9 o'clock and wound on through the main streets of the town. Plans had been set for the procession to go on to Pigeon Cove, another two

Figure 28. A View of Rockport from the highest slope of the Headlands. In the middle of the picture is T Wharf with the old coal pocket at its end.

miles, but the 90 degree heat was so oppressive, that several by-standers as well as participants suffered from sunstroke. As a result of the discomfort, the marchers shortened their route and turned toward the ocean breezes and Norwood's Head, where they found enormous tents, large enough to accommodate 600 people, and tables "laden with good things."

The fund-raisers had earned $600 to pay for the bands, fireworks, and a speaker, with military units, fraternal lodges in full regalia, and young people on decorated floats and carriages. In the afternoon, with paraders and guests refreshed, the program continued with a reading of the Declaration of Independence, and a patriotic speech that managed to hold the interest of listeners for another hour and a half. In the end, the day-long program was described as "a stirring extravaganza."

The expanding Norwood family now counted many owners of the common rights to Norwood's Head Pasture, rights that were called "six cow rights." This complex division of ownership, after several decades, led in 1890 to a court-appointed commission to devise a plan, (in 1890) with owners, to unite the entire parcel for development.

Figure 29. Looking east down Caleb's Lane in the 1930's

•••

The Great Wall • Old Garden Landing

•••

The territory now known as The Headlands was part of the original sixteen-acre grants allotted in 1708, some seventy-five years earlier. Old maps show the outline of a stone wall extending along the total boundary of the fourteen-acre Norwood's Head. Several deeds refer to the wall as a boundary, and much of the wall still exists today, constructed, as it was, of enormous glacial boulders. In New England, walls were not always boundaries. Sometimes they were rough-cast formations resulting from clearing the pasture land. It is possible that The Headlands wall was built to define the original Joseph Allen grant, perhaps to control the grazing cows and horses, or simply to mark off the property. The monumental Great Stone Wall may well be an historic symbol of the Norwood affinity for stone work, a link between the earliest Norwoods of Leckhampton Court and the rocky shores of Cape Ann on which they settled.

At some point in time, a pathway was extended southward from Atlantic Avenue, past the wall, to Caleb's Lane, and evidence remains that a portion of the wall was pushed aside at that time to make way for an extension of Atlantic Avenue. On the south side of the wall the narrow cart path, through a swampy expanse, eventually formed Caleb's Lane. The 1930 photograph shows the topography, before the swamp was filled in.

Someone has said, "A stone wall declares 'I was here.'" The stone wall at the Norwood Headlands echoes "I was here." While it does not reveal the exact date it was built, an 1819 deed, a part of the 1707 grant, mentions the wall. Other maps indicate construction in the early 1800s, when Caleb and his sons divided ownership. In any case, the wall of stones has been a part of

Figure 30. Looking west up Caleb's Lane (current view)

Figure 31. The Watering Place Old Garden Road

The Headlands scene for at least 200 years.

Around the point of The Headlands, and just south of Long Cove, stretched one of the six beaches surrounding Sandy Bay. Few clues were found to determine the origin of the name "Old Garden Beach." The name

Figure 32. Old Garden Beach in the late 1800s - looking South along the Old Garden Path.

appears to have been first used as early as 1708, when records show a "Garden Landing Place" and a "Cape Garden Beach." Over the years, some have theorized that the native Indians who had fished off the beach during the summer seasons, created gardens near their seasonal dwellings. (See Plate B) The soil of this upland area was extremely fertile, and water plentiful, as can be seen today in the watersheds flowing from both north and south to Caleb's Lane. Early grants refer to a stream and watering place near this "landing." First called Garden Landing Place, and later named Old Garden Beach, it is believed that the "Old Garden" received its name from the settlers who observed the Indian gardens in the area. Historians tell us that native Indians of that day traveled from Maine in the spring, cleared the dense growth of trees back a few feet from the shore, burned off tree stumps, and planted corn in the remaining rich soil. Native Indians taught Cape Anners that where trees were cleared the soil was especially productive for their gardens. While waiting for the corn to grow, they built huts, fished,

Figure 33. Very early photograph of Old Garden Beach. Note Straitsmouth Island lighthouse, far top right.

hunted for game, and with the autumn harvest they returned to their homes in the north.

The SBHS has a fine collection of Indian artifacts discovered in the vicinity of Old Garden Beach. In the year 1908 workmen on The Headlands unearthed two stone hammers, relics of early inhabitants or visiting Indians. Long in the possession of Jason Giles when he owned The Headlands, the two specimen stones are shaped for thongs to be bound to a handle and used much like a hammer. They are rare examples of an early tool which preceded the tomahawk. At the present parking lot near Old Garden Beach, leveled along the roadway for parking in 1900, workmen discovered fishing weights, a gouge, arrowheads, and an Indian garden hoe. Several of these objects have been preserved for viewing in the SBHS. The hoe seems to support the concept of gardens in the area.

Figure 34. An Indian hoe found at the Old GardenBeach - Headlands area.

The deed of Allen property in 1725 mentions a "Landing Place" (the beach) and a "Watering place and brook" within 165 feet of the landing place. The Old Garden Beach location indicates clearly the idea of fertile land for summer crops, nearby fishing, and a

Pasture land above Old Garden Beach. Note the stone walls reaching toward the sea, following the line of the 1708 Land Grants.

boat landing — all good reasons for the "Red Men" to establish a seasonal village. With these grants so conveniently located for the fishing interests, where once the "Red Men" had spent their summers, the sixteen lots of the Norwood sons were soon ready for the fishermen to build their houses.

Since moving back to Cape Ann from Attleboro in 1740, records show that the finances of the Norwood family had improved but slowly. A dozen years later, the Gloucester tax record listed Joshua Norwood at a zero assessment. However, some twenty years following word of Caleb's discovery, the Norwood assessment was listed as the highest in town, equal to the Sandy Bay Pier Company, with the single exception of the Pool family. The Norwood family, it appeared, had increased their finances in the community to more than the normal income of fishermen and granite workers. With many lots now assigned to the Norwood family, they were among the first to start building their houses, an activity reflecting a notable improvement in Norwood finances.

Figure 35. Caleb Norwood's first House 14 Atlantic Ave Built 1755

•••

Norwood Houses

•••

By the end of the year of 1772, Caleb's neighbors continued to whisper of his new-found wealth, but whether the rumors were true or not Caleb kept his secret. That is not to say, however, that he was idle during the eventful years of the new decade. Early in 1770, he had married his second wife, Jerusha, and only a few months into the next year, with rumors of his discovery of gold beginning to circulate, he had purchased the Headlands for 160 pounds and had moved his log cabin to its new location at Long Cove. At about the same time, both the Allen and Norwood families had managed to acquire large tracts of land along the shore where their harbor business had begun to grow. (See Plate F)

Caleb and Jerusha were already settled and living in a cape-style cottage on the Headlands property and a short distance from the log cabin. This cottage, built in 1755 on the Allen's Headlands property (now #14 Atlantic Avenue) though modest in size, Caleb and Jerusha must have found to be a great improvement over the crowded living conditions of a log cabin at Straitsmouth. The following year, around the corner and still on Norwood lots, the family built another house. This house began as a similar modest structure with its floors supported by logs cut from the property, but in the future it would undergo many changes. Eventually, this second house was moved back from the street, then turned halfway around, with two ells added to make it into a larger two-family structure. The long history of this house began with Attorney Henri Woods, who had married Marietta Norwood and later assisted in legal division of the property. The house was

Figure 36. Caleb Norwood's second House 39 Mount Pleasant St Built 1756

passed on to his heirs, then to William Norwood (Caleb's son) and his wife, Susanna Wheeler Norwood, and later still to their daughters. Many years later it became an inn and in more recent years was known as Charbury House. It was into this house, at the age of seventeen, that Susanna Norwood moved at her marriage, in 1843, to Solomon Torrey. Susanna was a daughter of Charles Norwood, a farmer, and a son of Caleb, Jr. Both her grandparents were Norwoods, and to confuse the family relationship still further, Caleb, Jr. married a cousin of his step-mother, Jerusha, with the same name of Jerusha. Susanna and Solomon started their married life together on a third floor addition built for Susanna by her maternal grandparents, William and Susanna Wheeler Norwood.

In the years that followed the building of Charbury House, both the Allen and the Norwood families had managed to acquire even more sizable tracts of land, but the War for Independence now intervened to take whatever funds Cape Anners had to spare.

During the Revolution, stories of Caleb's gold mingled with tales of pirates still seeking protection in Cape Ann coves. But, by the time the Declaration of Independence had been signed, all the old rumors had taken on an added dimension. With the turn of a new decade (1780) tales were

Figure 37. Caleb Norwood Jr's House 37 Mount Pleasant St (Cove Hill Inn) 1791

spreading of a certain gold ring. The ring, it was said, had been made from a bar of Caleb's gold, as a gift to his wife, Jerusha. Since no jewelry factories or stores yet existed, few believed the new rumors, but when it was learned that a factory for making jewelry was actually established in Attleboro, Caleb's birthplace, the amazing coincidence took on a new significance. The first and only jewelry manufacturing in the new country, although short-lived, was established in Attleboro in 1780, the year the new rumors had started. The truth of this rumor has never been proven, the ring never found, but the search and the rumors go on.

To Caleb's neighborhood, impoverished by the Revolution, he appeared to be on a spending spree, but it was not until 1791 that the Norwood family began to build more houses. On a lot between the old log cabin and the house at 39 Mt. Pleasant Street then owned by William, with the family's improved finances, Caleb, Jr. built a manor house for himself and Jerusha, later to be inherited by their son, Charles. (This house later became known as the Tresnon House, and is presently Cove Hill Inn.)

Not long after the marriage of Susanna and Solomon, at the urging of his father, Solomon had departed with ten other young men from Cape Ann, to seek his fortune in the rush for California gold. Susanna was left at home,

Figure 38. Major Francis Norwood House 10 Atlantic Ave 1797

not only without Solomon but with the grief of losing their first child. Before he left, Solomon had gotten out of the stone business but he had not gotten it out of his mind. He wrote to Susanna describing the ruins of Panama that he saw enroute to California. "It is a city entirely walled in with stone and cement. The houses and rich churches are built of stone and richly ornamented with well cut statuary all tumbled down and going to ruin."

During the period of Solomon's absence, Susanna moved back from her grandparents' home to her parents' home, next door, at 37 Mt. Pleasant Street. It was here that Susanna began to write in her diary the day-to-day routine of living without Solomon. Her first paragraph stated that John Quincy Adams had died February 28, 1848, an entry perhaps indicative of Solomon's background and interest in the Quincy quarries. This two-story house with its seventeen rooms eventually became known as the Tresnon House when Susanna's daughter, also named Susanna, married Charles Tresnon.

When Caleb died, in 1814, he left a fourteen-acre Headlands lot nearest the sea to his three sons —Caleb, Jr., William, and ("Major") Francis. Charles inherited the house at 37 Mt. Pleasant Street where Susanna resided in Solomon's absence.

Figure 39. Gorham Norwood House High and School Streets 1812

Another house, at 10 Atlantic Avenue, built in 1797 on a piece of this seashore property for "Major" Francis Norwood, later became the property of Artist Harrison Cady, famous illustrator of "Peter Rabbit."

Meanwhile, yet one more "mansion" was built, for Gorham Norwood, another son of Caleb, on the corner of High Street and School Street, and later sold to Hosea Tufts.

Figure 40. Ornamental Wrought Iron Gate Entrance to the Torrey Stone House

Susanna Norwood Torrey

Although members of the Norwood family continued to build on the surrounding acres, it was the beautiful Susanna Norwood Torrey, living at 37 Mt. Pleasant Street, who provided the romance in the family saga.

By the year 1850, Solomon Torrey had returned from California, and though he recorded no wealth from his five-year absence, he and Susanna were able to build their own house on Norwood Avenue. They built a "cottage" of stone. If Susanna had inherited the family affinity for stone work, she and Solomon also drew upon Solomon's skills from working in his father's granite quarries on Granite Street, work that had been profitable for the family.

"Solomon considers himself a stone dealer," Susanna wrote in her diary, "and he finds expression in his stone work." The house they built is noted for the artistic design of its beautiful stonework and its wrought-iron gateway. As they began to take account of their finances for building their house, Susanna wrote in her diary that Solomon "drew forth from a straw bed, several long bundles containing gold in ten dollar pieces, then a pocketbook with several hundred in bills--$1200 in all," savings that Susanna had forgotten about. Susanna's notation, undisclosed for so many years, presents the possibility that it was a share of her grandfather's gold.

Artists were even then beginning to come to Cape Ann, and when Susanna was only seventeen years of age, one artist, Alfred J. Wiggin, had already made a name for himself as an artist of portraits in primitive style. Artist Wiggin not only fell in love with the beautiful Susanna, he painted her

Figure 41. The Stone Cottage of Solomon and Susanna Torrey Norwood Ave 1850

portrait. With the painting nearly finished, the young Solomon Torrey, a friend of the artist, had admired the portrait and the attractive young woman who posed for it. Solomon asked to meet her.

Meanwhile, Joseph Allen, Jr. and his wife, friendly neighbors with a penchant for matchmaking, sought to encourage a love affair between the artist and the lovely Susanna. One day they invited Susanna to walk with them and collect moss in the Norwood pasture. On the walk they found "an abundance," they said, then walked on to the shore "having a gay time," when Mrs. Allen suggested that Susanna might return Alfred's interest in her. Susanna considered him "conceited" and showed little interest until he brought Solomon, one day, to meet her. Alfred Wiggin tried to break up the match but failed, and he rarely called upon Susanna after that meeting. Susanna and Solomon were said to have had a happy, though brief, married life together.

While Solomon was away in California Susanna recorded for him, in her diary, the day-to-day events, and when he returned from California, and they began to build their own stone house, Susanna continued to record these daily activities. "Solomon attended an auction in Gloucester," she wrote in April. "He bought peach, plum, pear, cherry, and apple trees." A few weeks later in the spring she wrote, "Solomon went to Boston and bought asparagus roots, four grape vines, and two pear trees. They cost him $3 for which he got laughed at." Another time she wrote, " Solomon is busy splitting stones to build a shed."

Solomon and Susanna had two daughters, Susanna, who married Charles Tresnon, an Englishman, and Aria, who married Ben Haskell; but Solomon's life was short—he lived a brief five years in the stone house that he had built. One more poignant entry in Susanna's diary was written in August 1856 not long before his death.

Figure 42. Needlepoint by Susanna Norwood Torrey

"I went out to take a little walk with mother and Ora (sister) and as we came along home we met Mr. John Parsons who invited us into his garden." (At the northeast corner of School Street and Pleasant Street, a road having been laid out for travel from Gott Street across Pleasant Street, through Andrew Lane's pasture at Prospect Street, in the 1830s and 40s.) It was an area that Susanna remembered as a rough pasture and brier patch, but she wrote in her diary, "The tall trees looked invitingly over the high fence and as we entered the garden gate, the branches of the plum heavy with fruit bent gracefully over our head. It was a beautiful prospect for us. The trees were thickly set in rows and heavy laden with fruit of various colors and kinds. Everything looked as if it had received particular care. We walked to and fro through its many paths continually coming upon something to excite our admiration. I never saw such an abundance of plums. Some little trees not so high as my head bent beneath their burden of fruit. Every spot seemed turned to good account. Upon the outskirts of the garden was a large rock over which was built an arbor and upon this was trained a grape vine. Since my remembrance this was a wild pasture covered only with rocks and brambles. This little Eden has been the work of a few years and his own hands have done it all. He seemed pleased with our call

Figure 43. One of Susanna's scrapbooks, containing graceful designs of the dried mosses in their natural colors, is preserved at the SBHS. A sample dried design is shown above.

and gave us a polite invitation to come again when the fruit is ripe."

Susanna's interest in gathering mosses on her pasture walks extended to gathering sea mosses along the shore as well. One of her favorite pastimes was drying specimens of these plants and making prints of them in a scrap book.

She learned from Joseph Allen how to prepare sea mosses for drying. "Take them home, put in water, and select the most beautiful specimens,"he advised her. "Then immerse once again," he continued, "with the paper upon which to dry them." Following Joseph's teaching, Susanna would then stretch the paper and carefully lay out the delicate branches of her collection.

Susanna spent many happy hours along the shore, as well as in the fields and swamps, searching for the perfect specimens for her artistic arrangements. In April 1848, she wrote in her diary, "Busily engaged in arranging some very beautiful mosses and dried grasses, on a pasteboard frame, in which I succeeded to my satisfaction." The next day, still feeling satisfied with her collection of mosses and grasses, she wrote "I am employed on this beautiful spring morning in making a moss basket."

Susanna appreciated, too, the beauties of the landscape that surrounded her, and one day she wrote of Gully Cove. " The Gully, with its unpoetical name, will soon be mentioned with the things that were. At one time twenty feet deep, five feet wide, and ninety feet long, during a storm last year the outer end was broken away by force of the waves, and a large piece of stone, weighing fifty tons, was precipitated into the lower end open to the sea."

On April 10, 1848, Susanna recorded for history that the first load of cotton had arrived for the Annisquam Cotton Mill, and nine days later she noted that a surprise snow storm blanketed Cape Ann on the day that Solomon severed his connection with his father's stone business.

Although Susanna began her marriage as a naive young teenager, she lived a long life of service to her community. According to Rockport historians Marshall Swan and Merrill McLane, she not only offered her services as an auditor for fund-raising committees but, in 1870 she became the first woman to serve as treasurer of the Universalist Society, formed thirty years earlier. Though some members disapproved of the choice of a woman as treasurer, McLane noted, the pastor supported Womens' Rights. Once again there was so much ill feeling in the town that churchgoers were forced to snuff out the candles and lock the church doors for a time. Many members of the Norwood family were also active in this society, including Caleb, Sr., Caleb, Jr., Francis, Jr. and William, all of whom were civic minded and active in almost all aspects of the town's business.

Figure 44. The Bowling Alley House after being divided and moved to 36 Atlantic Ave

Division of Headlands Property

For several decades before the 1900s, the Headlands property had already been under consideration as ideal for development for summer cottages or hotels, but the many owners precluded any division acceptable to all. Finally, the planners conceded, it was probably impossible to get a consent from all the owners to divide the land without the legal process of endless court settlements.

At this point Jason Giles stepped in and began to acquire titles to the lots, one by one, for ownership and control of the property. Jason Giles was born in Sandy Bay in 1830. He married Delphina Norwood, granddaughter of "Major" Francis Norwood. (She also had a brother named Francis). Jason was forty years old when he set his sights on the Headlands property with plans for its future use uppermost in his mind. Fortunately, his plans included restrictions on the lots to enable citizens of the town to enjoy the beauty of this section of the town. In later years his daughter, Hattie Bass, generously agreed to sell this granite outcrop, known as the Headlands, at a price the town could afford to buy and use as a park for the pleasure of future generations.

The total purchase of "Norwood's Pasture" would include a small lot southeast of what had become known as "The Bowling Alley Property." This house and lot, incidentally, was never used as a bowling alley, but was a long, low structure resembling a bowling alley. The Bowling Alley house, located at what is now the intersection of Norwood Avenue and Atlantic Avenue, was built in the 1860s and planned as a summer cottage for Feducia Norwood, daughter of William. When Feducia agreed to sell her property to

Figure 45. Current view of the Rudder Grange 36 Atlantic Ave

Giles in 1870, she signed off her deed of ownership "for one dollar and other valuable considerations." Eight gable dormer windows stood out from each side of the structure and when Jason Giles purchased the building he split it into two cottages which were then moved to an adjacent lot on Atlantic Avenue. This division of the house was designed to make way for an extension of Norwood Avenue to be laid out as a main road to the Headlands development. Giles named the resulting two summer cottages "The Anchorage" and "The Rudder" and for several years he rented them to summer tourists. Eventually the southern cottage was torn down while the north building remains today on Atlantic Avenue. (See Plate E)

Jason Giles proceeded with surveys and a bold plan to develop an expanse of avenues that measured 40 feet in width and 4000 feet in length. Meanwhile, the town of Rockport cooperated with him and his plan, agreeing to extend the water supply and place hydrants for fire protection. In return, Giles promised that electric lights were soon to follow, all within easy access—"a five minute walk," he advertised, to the center of town, as well as to the beaches and shore. His sales advertising called attention to the nearby Old Garden Beach for swimming, and the outcrop of rocks for fishing. As for a variety of scenery there was no equal; "superior," he claimed, "to anything on the North Shore." And above all else, Giles assured his potential

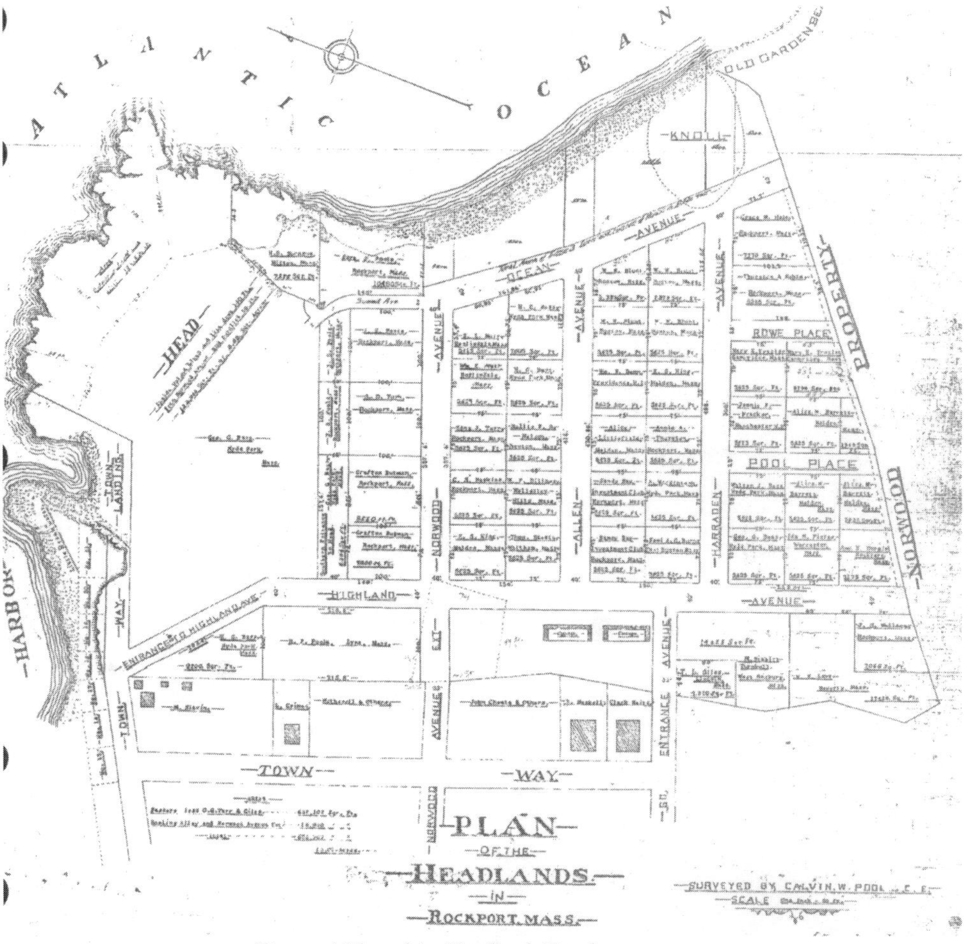

Figure 46. Plan of the Headlands Development 1909

buyers, "The air must pass over the ocean and therefore be cooled and purified from all objectionable features."

But there was one "objectionable" feature not to be overlooked. One Norwood owner, Olive Tarr, daughter of William, owned a share near the Great Stone Wall, and she refused to sign off her share. Feeling that Giles was trying to take advantage of her, she and her daughter remained adamant in their refusal.

In June 1898 officials appointed by the Probate Court of Essex County eleven years earlier notified lot owners of a hearing to be held for the partition of the Norwood Pastures real estate. Notices were sent to Henri Woods, Zeno A. Appleton, Heirs of Charles Tarr, Thaddeus Giles, Heirs of

Commissioners' Notice.

To Henri N. Woods, Zeno A. Appleton, Heirs of Charles Tarr, Thaddeus Giles, Heirs of Oresa Tarr, Olive Tarr, Ella Low and Charles M. Wright, *Greeting:*

You are hereby notified that the subscribers have been appointed by the Hon. Rollin E. Harmon, Judge of Probate for the County of Essex, to make partition of the real estate owned by the persons above named, situate in the town of Rockport, and known as the Norwood's Pasture, containing fourteen acres $\frac{3}{10}$, more or less, bounded Northerly by the land of the Sandy Bay Pier Company, and Easterly by the sea, Southerly by land of heirs of Caleb Norwood, Westerly by land formerly of Addison Gott, Charles H. Clark and others. And that Thursday, the twenty-third day of June, A. D. 1898, at 2 o'clock P. M., at the rooms of the Granite Savings Bank, in said Rockport, is the time and place fixed for hearing all parties interested therein, at which time and place you may be present.

CALVIN W. POOL, } *Surviving*
NATHANIEL RICHARDSON, } *Commissioners.*

Rockport, June 16, 1898.

Figure 47. Commissioners' Notice to meet with lawyers, Rockport 1898

Oresa Tarr, Ella Low, Charles Wright, and Olive Tarr. The largest owner was Henri Woods, the smallest owner listed was Thaddeus Giles, one of several Norwood-Giles cousins.

The property was described as having fourteen acres more or less, with land owned by Sandy Bay Pier Company on the north, the Atlantic Ocean on the east, heirs of Caleb Norwood to the south, and the western boundary shared by Addison Gott, Charles Clark, and others. All interested parties were requested to meet on June 23, 1898, at the Granite Savings Bank, an institution incorporated in 1853, forty-five years earlier. After several hours of deliberation, no agreement was reached that day and the meeting adjourned to July 7.

At the June and July meetings, a number of plans to divide the property were offered for consideration by each owner. Finally, after many lengthy discussions, a plan was drawn up and accepted by all except Henri Woods, who said that he found so much ill will existing among the owners that he could not accept the plan.(Henri was married to Marietta Norwood, Susanna's maternal aunt.)

Correspondence followed between Giles and the heirs involved, and he now sought further legal advice over the disagreements. The idea then occurred to Giles and his attorneys to form a company of shareholders in an attempt to make the property more marketable. The owners agreed to this plan. "My object," Giles told them, "was to secure a part for a cottage site. I did not dream (as some had suggested) of holding more of the property." Zeno Appleton, one owner, also sought legal advice and to his dismay found that Henri Woods was in a position to delay division of the property indefinitely. This disheartening situation came close to being solved when Howard Pool of Lynn offered to sell his one sixteenth share. Appleton accepted Pool's offer, with Giles agreeing to buy the other half of the lot, and once again the other owners agreed to the plan.

The problem, however, was not yet solved. The day after what some owners believed was a final agreement, Everett Lane offered Giles one half of a one-twelfth share, owned by F.E. Lane, which Giles agreed to buy. The price was a little less than he had paid Appleton, so Giles accepted the proposition for both lots. He then asked all parties to meet him at the office of Henri Woods to sign the deeds. All agreed to be present except Olive Tarr, who lived in Dorchester and had been notified by letter.

As soon as they arrived at the meeting, it was immediately evident that the old ill feeling still lingered among some of the shareholders. George T. Tarr, although he had earlier expressed his support for the plan, now refused to join the signers "as long as Henri Woods holds an interest." Tarr's actions were so outrageous to Giles and so revolting to the other shareholders that Giles concluded the group would be better off without him, and so offered to buy out Tarr's share. Tarr accepted the Giles offer, a one- fifteenth share.

This agreement, however, was far from settling the long-standing conflicts. The heirs of Captain Charles Tarr (Albert Tarr and George E. Tarr) agreed to sign as soon as they consulted with a brother-in-law and co-heir, Mr. Wheeler. "Albert Tarr," Giles wrote to one heir, "has promised to sign at three different times, but instead of carrying out his promise, he told Olive Tarr's daughter, Geneva, that I was taking advantage of them. He so convinced Geneva that she was able to influence her mother. 'Don't have anything to do with it, Mother,' the daughter advised. 'It is a case of the Big Fish eating up the Little Fish.'"

The June meeting adjourned without the matter being settled. There then ensued a series of correspondence between Giles in Gloucester and Olive Tarr in Dorchester. Twenty letters stretched the matter out until October, without progress in obtaining the final signature for division of the property. Back in July, Olive Tarr had assented to one plan, but then, at the urging of her daughter, had backed out on her agreement. At first agreeing to the plan, with Giles in a position to take over the shares owned by A.W. Tarr and Henri Woods, Olive Tarr withdrew her first acceptance of the plan, leaving Giles with a possible loss of $2900, as he said, "deeper in the mire."

Giles then patiently tried another method of approaching Olive Tarr. He hired one of the officials who had been appointed by the Probate Court to present the case to her and try to convince her that the final proposal made good sense. The new proposition made no effect on Olive Tarr, and Giles was obliged to pay for the services of the officer.

More weeks of frustrating delays followed, extending to late October, when Olive Tarr made a trip to Rockport "to view the premises." At that time, Giles offered to set off a piece of land that would be equivalent to her share, along with the previous offer to buy her out for cash plus a bonus of $133.33 over the original offer. She lingered in Rockport for two days, during which time Giles "entertained" her, hired a carriage for her to go and view the Norwood Head Pasture, then escorted her to a Justice of the Peace and promised to assume all expenses for a legal agreement, signature, and deed for the property. In order to make the transition easier for Olive Tarr, Giles and the officials requested her to have her husband on hand when they would go to Boston for their final signatures. With all arrangements made, however, Olive's Tarr's husband was not at home to receive the delegation of officers, the time limit had more than expired, and Olive Tarr once more went back on her word.

By this time Giles had reached the end of his patience. He instructed his attorney to bring action for his losses of time and money. Frequent discussions then continued for the remainder of the year. Now a narrow strip of land, between her land and Highland Avenue, was brought into the discussion and Giles bought it from her. Giles furthermore agreed to take over all costs of building the avenues, with no charges to her. She was to be deeded "Right in Common" to all reservations, free of all construction and maintenance costs. Still not quite satisfied, Olive Tarr continued to question the acreage but in the end it was revealed that her share of costs amounted to $.02 per square foot while the cost for Giles, after putting in the Avenues, would amount to $.025 per square foot.

Early in January 1901 when Giles and his attorneys finally settled the long-standing disputes, Giles wrote to Olive Tarr's daughter, "Has the Big Fish ate up the Little Fish, or the reverse that the Little Fish has ate up the Big Fish?"

The deal for ownership of the Norwood Headlands was finally closed, its northern approach, Atlantic Avenue, following the harbor.

Figure 48. Contemporary view of Rockport Harbor.

Norwood Interests At Long Cove

The fourteen-acre piece of the Norwood Headlands nearest the shore, with the Great Stone Wall forming its southern and western boundaries, remained in the hands of the younger Norwoods--Caleb, Jr., William, and Francis, all sons of Caleb ("Red Cap)" who died in 1814. Already their maritime interests and investments in boats had expanded their shipping and trading activities. By 1800, with fishing profitable at that time, seventy boats overcrowded Long Cove, tied to the mooring stones built at Straitsmouth by their grandfather, Joshua.

During the first thirty-five years of the 1800s, the Norwoods built a wharf on the southern shore of Long Cove, Bearskin Neck, in order to accommodate their increasing number of boats for fishing and trading. At the same time they also acquired several fish houses and as one historian wrote, "Quite a track of flake room."

As early as 1746, Ebenezer Pool had built a second wharf on his own grant but these structures, built of timber and stone, were too frail to withstand the many northeast storms, and they lasted only a few years. These two wharves received minor repairs and by 1800 were useless as protection for the harbor.

In 1809, the Sandy Bay Pier Company organized in an attempt to provide the harbor with protection from storm damage and therefore make it more serviceable for the fishermen. The new enterprise sold 600 shares of their corporation at one dollar a share, and forty-five fishermen signed the agreement. Their expectations were to build a protective wharf on the west-

Figure 49. T Wharf at low tide. Behind the grounded vessels is the old coal pocket.

erly flats, with pay for construction going to the treasurer in either money or labor. In 1811, they began to build the wharf and two years later they continued their successful venture with a second wharf, but in 1819, a mere six years after they were built, severe storm damage once again took its toll on both wharves. Disheartened by the destruction after their efforts, at great sacrifice, to provide shelter for their boats, a surveyor reported "the condition of the wharves now very poor and greatly crippled."

In another ten years, although the number of fishing vessels had diminished to forty, harbor conditions were still so cramped that it was possible to walk on the deck of vessels, from one damaged wharf to another. Although 1828 was reported as "a good mackerel year," the Sandy Bay Pier Company was unable to remedy the situation without financial aid from other sources.

In January 1826 the Sandy Bay Pier Company had voted "to build a wharf from the road down toward the water to cover the ledge in the basin." This was the beginning of the T Wharf, which fanned out to make the T at the water's edge. Later a coal pocket stored fuel for the cotton mill. The south side was later leased as "The Cold Storage," for fish preservation, but in 1930 became the Sandy Bay Yacht Club.

In the spring of 1832, the Sandy Bay Pier Company invited all fishermen to assemble at the Proprietor's School and express their views on ways

Figure 50. The old coal pocket was replaced by the Interstate Fish Corporation. After it was destroyed by a fire in 1923 it was succeeded by the Sandy Bay Yacht Club

to protect the harbors. As a result of this meeting, the Sandy Bay Pier Company, with renewed organization and enthusiasm, petitioned the Legislature for an Act of Authority "to purchase, take and hold, all the lands and flats and privileges for a safe and convenient harbor at Long Cove." The desired property as listed included the Headlands, Atlantic Avenue, the shore side of Dock Square, and all of Bearskin Neck, within certain bounds, beginning at Norwood Head, so called, a sufficient distance from the bank for a good cartway; "thence westerly," a detailed list continued, "to a bend in William Norwood's field wall; thence across said field to the upper bar post on the opposite side of the field; thence to the southern side of the road by the Widow Norwood's barn; thence continue by southerly side of the road to Caleb Norwood's red house; thence by said house through the porch to fifteen feet southerly of the end of said road where it comes to the highway; thence northwesterly by highway to Eleazer Boynton's land; thence northeasterly by said Boynton's land to the east corner of same; thence west-northerly by land of Boynton, E. Oakes, John Gott, and others, to north corner of same; thence southwesterly by land of Oakes and others to highway; thence northerly by the highway until it comes to 50 feet distant from the slaughterhouse lot; thence northeasterly 30 feet; thence northwesterly 50 feet, until it comes to a slaughterhouse lot and George Denison's land to a road; thence by said road and George Denison's land to highway; thence northerly by the highway to Widow Norwood's land; thence northerly by said Tarr's land to corner of same; thence northwesterly and other courses by land of Sally Tarr, George Denison, Samuel McJennet, Daniel Thurston, John Burns, and Thomas O. Marshall and Company, and also including all the land northeasterly, commonly called Bearskin Neck."

With the property now clearly defined, in order to begin acquisition of the land the Sandy Bay Pier Company first appointed a committee and instructed its members to purchase as much real estate as possible from private owners. At this meeting, the committee was also instructed to make a plan of Bearskin Neck, on the north side of Long Cove, and advised to run a line from Allen's Head (Norwood's Head but still called by some "Allen's Head") to the highway that "would match bounds in the act of possession."

The following year, the committee voted to proceed to take over the real estate as the company had outlined. At the same time, the committee began discussions for a possible legal separation between Gloucester and its fifth parish, Sandy Bay. However, the committee had as many disagreements as Jason Giles had had with the Norwood divisions of the same property, and they excused themselves from further deliberations.

Continued study of early transactions of the Pier Company revealed that Lucy Norwood, widow of William, transferred, on November 30, 1844, twelve shares of Sandy Bay Pier Company stock to Francis, four shares to Seth, and four shares to William, Jr., with the conditions that annual income from the shares go to her for her lifetime.

By 1873, The Sandy Bay Pier Company was still buying and selling lots without much profit. By 1884, it became necessary for the Pier Company to consider, once again, improvement in Long Cove from much accumulated storm damage. With dissension continuing among committee members, they eventually reorganized and resumed discussions for taking over the real estate surrounding Long Cove as well as ongoing talk of a breakwater to make a genuine harbor out of the already "Long" Cove. But their problems, at times, seemed almost insurmountable. Not only were rents long overdue for wharf space, but their inability to collect some fees for ice deliveries at T Wharf had become a serious issue. Then there were

Figure 52. Fish Shacks on Star Island

what the Pier Company considered the excessively high taxes levied by the town, and of course the constant repairs due to storm damage. At one meeting, when the question arose as to liability as a result of a recent winter storm, inspectors of the damage reported, "If we were in your place we would not lose sleep over it." Negotiations for funding harbor repairs and buying up the Headlands property went on year after year, but when the deal to acquire the land was finally agreed upon and signed, all the stone for the breakwater was quarried in Sandy Bay, and funded by the government at a cost of $190,000.

The Pier Company negotiations of the lots continued on both north (Bearskin Neck) and south sides of Long Cove, but in 1840 all marketing of the lots had ceased. On that date, Sandy Bay separated from Gloucester and incorporated, with Pigeon Cove, under the name of Rockport. With the old Sandy Bay now incorporated as Rockport, the original Sandy Bay Pier Company voted to liquidate its assets and to dispose among the stockholders all surplus property. They proceeded to appraise the property and then to sell the lots at auction on December 12, 1843, the auction to be held in the Sail Loft at Bearskin Neck.

After the evaluation and sales of lots on the north side of Long Cove, Bearskin Neck, they went on to settle all accounts including stone, wood, ironwork, labor, and the hiring of oxen and blacksmiths. In the end they counted a surplus in their treasury of $2566.04. Three months later, in the spring of 1844, with their accounts settled, they lost no time in looking after their other business interests. They sternly directed all persons who had stumps and mooring stones in Long Cove to remove them forthwith, "in order to clear the water passage of encumbrances," or "face indictment before the Grand Jury!" Note: Stumps were oak trees divested of limbs and branches, with the root retained.

The harbor business went on with routine duties, always with the fear of storms threatening to destroy the wharves that the new town of Rockport had been able to build or restore. In April 1851 a heavy northeast gale pummeled the harbor for three days, causing an exceedingly high tide. This storm resulted in extensive damage to the old wharf and the breakwater at the entrance to Long Cove. The stockholders, ever watchful of their expenses for keeping the T Wharf in repair, voted to spend a sum of money, not to exceed $100, to extend the seawall at Long Cove, toward Norwood's wharf. Some stones of this wharf remain visible today, at the far end of Atlantic Avenue.

During the years of selling off the lots at Bearskin Neck, sales had also included talk about lots along Atlantic Avenue, on the south side of Long Cove where Norwood boat owners had moored their vessels for more than a hundred years. At the time of the Giles purchase of the Headlands, considerable discussion went on concerning these lots, resulting in a survey and laying out of lots with a fifty-foot frontage, and followed by a decision to sell these lots, too, at public auction.

Research of old agreements made when Gloucester owned the land, and a survey of the premises, brought to light twenty-two lots in all, including the Landing at Norwood's Head, and a description of the way that led from Mt. Pleasant Street to these lots. These lots all led to the old Norwood "Landing Place" in Long Cove, known as Star Island. This landmark close to shore was little more than a mound of rocks, but large enough for Norwoods to build three shacks for storing their fishing gear. Star Island with its foundation of rock, but exposed to centuries of storms, finally succumbed to the great storm of 1978, and gave back to the sea its old "Landing Place." Only a

Figure 53. Margeson Studio on the left and a fish house now one residence on Atlantic Ave

row of rocks remain to mark where the Norwood brothers moored their vessels. In 1877, owners of the Norwood Headlands had made a request to the Board of Selectmen to put up a "Private Way" notice at the opening of the street (Atlantic Avenue) leading to Norwood's Head. One lot they reserved for a road between two of the lots, to be measured as fifteen feet wide, and set off as a way to the beach. The lots were to be laid out to a depth of thirty-six feet, and of varying width. The twenty- one lots were sold, with the one reserved for a way as the committee required.

After viewing the lots to be sold, they voted that none of them should be sold at auction for less than four cents per foot. The auction was set for July 1, 1899, and ads were placed in *The Breeze*, *The Gloucester Daily Times*, and *The Review*, as well as in Boston newspapers—"at an expense," they said, "not to exceed $10."

Fair weather favored them for a good attendance at the sale on July 1, and the bidding was as good as the weather. The earliest artist to come to Rockport and establish a permanent home expressed an interest in one of the lots along Atlantic Avenue. Gilbert Tucker Margeson bought lot #10, with a house on it, for $192.15. He later bought the adjoining lot and built a stone house for his studio. Margeson had studied art in France for a time, and the style of his stone cottage on the edge of Long Cove bears a striking resemblance to the studio of the French artist, Rousseau, who had received recognition in the art world at that time. All twenty-one lots were sold, with the one reserved for a way as the committee required.

Reports of the success of the auction were delayed for unexplained reasons, but after two years reasons for the delay came to light. It was reported that "certain parties" had questioned the legality of the titles, and now had sued the corporation. At a special meeting, called to determine a course of action, a director reviewed some of the history of the lots at Long Cove. "In the year 1800, one hundred years ago," he told his listeners, "there were 60 to 80 fishing vessels in the harbor." He went on to describe the extensive storm damage that had accumulated over the years, and he estimated that the fishing business had dwindled to one tenth of what it had once been. And in words disheartening to the fishermen of Long Cove, he warned them, "The large mackerel boats no longer come to this port."

Recurrent discussions of ownership, repairs, and improvements to the Long Cove wharf area went on for years with little progress until 1935. By this time the waterfront property of the reorganized Sandy Bay Pier Company had been assessed at $10,000. Money for the town to purchase this property was appropriated at town meeting in March 1935. The deed was signed in October and at this time the T Wharf area passed from individual ownership to become the property of the Town of Rockport.

Inns and Taverns

The Norwoods were not only mariners, fishermen, farmers, property owners, and held various town offices, but they were entrepreneurs. One at least, William, was a manufacturer of isinglass. Francis, Jr. was a member of the first fire company, Caleb, Jr. formed a partnership for cutting ice from Cape Pond, and several of the Norwood men invented methods of salting and curing the fish they caught. Caleb, Jr. found a way to make use of seaweed as a fertilizer for their rocky and unproductive soil. The Norwood women, too, the two Susannas, Lucy, and Mary among them, were often independent and active in their community.

In addition to all these varied interests, the Norwood family, since their arrival in Saugus in 1657, had maintained an interest and shrewd business sense in the management of inns and taverns. Taverns began at Sandy Bay as "Public Houses," according to Historian Ebenezer Pool, where some of the men "kept tavern," gathering in their own homes for an evening of social exchange, with the infallible rule of going home at nine o'clock. Early in the 1800s, twelve homes and shops held licenses as innkeepers and retailers of spirituous liquors. The rules for granting licenses were as strict as their own rules for going home on time, with the General Court providing forms for applicants to complete and return to the selectmen. At first applications for licenses were spasmodic, but the rules soon settled into a pattern to be enforced. The law required selectmen to decide on the number "necessary for receiving and refreshing travelers and strangers, and to serve on public occasions for the public good." Some were denied approval if a disturbance occurred on their premises. Francis and William Norwood were among the first to receive licenses as retailers, and Mary Norwood was one of the first women to be approved for an innkeeper's license.

At Pigeon Cove, in 1805, Captain Daniel Wheeler built a "tavern house" for his own living quarters, and for almost fifty years it was known as the Village Tavern. He was a fisherman but in a short time, having been active in the militia, he became the commanding officer of the local militia and thereafter he was known as an innkeeper. He was first commissioned as an Ensign, then advanced to Lieutenant, and then advanced again to Captain. He retired from the tavern business in 1838 but rented the business to William Norwood until 1846. At that time the tavern was turned over to Daniel Wheeler, Jr. and William Norwood opened his own tavern as the Pigeon Cove House.

Caleb Norwood purchased a building (the present Masonic building) and expanded it to be used as an inn for several years before selling to the Annisquam Cotton Mills, but even after this sale it was used for a time as an inn.

The Punch Bowl Tavern, one of the earliest and built in 1775, now a tourist shop and no longer a tavern, sits among the fishing shacks of Bearskin Neck. Three other taverns stand out as historic landmarks of the tavern industry and forerunners of the modern tourist industry. Five years after the building of the Punch Bowl Tavern, the Headland Tavern opened for business on the opposite side of Long Cove. One early visitor at this tavern was William Dean Howells, novelist, editor of the Atlantic Monthly, and friend of Mark Twain. At one time he aspired to buy the Headlands Tavern and tried to convince his wife of the advantages of living with a view of Sandy Bay harbor. Unfortunately, on the day she came to view the premises, an exceptionally low tide created an unpleasant stench of decaying fish on Atlantic Avenue, and the writer never purchased the property. However, the artist Harrison Cady later bought and restored the old inn, when he realized there was space for socializing in what he called the "common room."

One more tavern, although no longer used for that purpose, is still called The Old Tavern. Now owned by the Rockport Art Association, the original structure was once a one-story gambrel-roof house used first as a tavern and then sold to Caleb Norwood, Jr., who restored it for many uses, first as an inn, then by additions it became a drugstore and later on a restaurant. In time, a second floor was added and converted to a dance hall. As if

Figure 54. Rockport Art Association

all these uses were not enough for the old tavern, it was also a stopping place for the stage on its regular trips from Salem to Rockport. But in 1929, rooms in the tavern, with some of its ten fireplaces removed, found a new and permanent function.

The old Norwood tavern became the home of the Rockport Art Association, who acquired it for a purchase price of $6000. Art had replaced alcohol in the Norwood Tavern. Local architects removed the old fireplaces, remodeled the building, and art took over, making show rooms and meeting rooms for the purpose of furthering the interest in art that artists Margeson, Cady, Wiggin and others had started in another century. Art had replaced the taverns but inns were there to stay for them and for the tourists who were choosing, for their vacations, the same Cape Ann that Champlain, John Smith, and Francis Norwood had chosen in an earlier time.

Final Words From the Great StoneWall

The search for answers to the mystery of the Great Stone Wall had spanned many generations. The wall of stone remained in its place, as solid as when it had been built at Norwood's Head more than two centuries earlier. For many months Peter and Don had listened to the story told by the stones. "Have we left any stone unturned?" these persistent searchers wondered.

Their search had taken them back to the England of 1657, when the first Francis Norwood had set sail for the Cape Ann shore. Since then they had followed the Norwood family through uncounted generations. They had uncovered long forgotten records and found them reliable enough to assure that members of the Norwood family had built the Great Wall. They believed construction of the wall dated back at least to the year 1800. But where did the enormous stones come from?

Cape Ann, the searchers found, was buried under glacial ice for thousands of years. Over those centuries, melting and movement of the ice had gradually worked the stones to the surface. The ocean had played its part as well, with tides easily carrying great boulders inland from the shore, where men struggled to move them, sometimes to tidy up the landscape, but often to serve as boundaries for land owners, or to contain cattle, or to make way for a cart path or road.

Answers to their questions had been slow in coming. For the most part, living at Sandy Bay, the Norwood men were mariners of one kind or another. Some fished, others were businessmen who traded the fish for salt, sugar, and other supplies not available in the new land. Some fought in the

War for Independence. Some began to build boats, to broaden the markets for their fish, and some invented ways to make their fishing easier. Joshua Norwood had made mooring stones for tying up their boats.

They were civic-minded men and women who sat on committees to make decisions for their community, first to divide the land on which they had settled, then to settle disputes of later generations. Both men and women opened inns and taverns for overnight comfort of travelers, as well as drink and refreshment for day trippers. They built houses for their own comfort, and when adversaries threatened they stood their ground with courage, offering both their money and their lives. They cleared the land of trees and stumps, planted crops and fruit trees, and to their surprise discovered they could sell the very stone they found under their feet.

They had made good use of the fish, the timber, and the granite. Only one more piece of the Norwood puzzle remained. Had they satisfied the doubters? Had they found sufficient proof of Caleb Norwood's treasure in gold? Furthermore, had their searching convinced the scoffers? Having convinced themselves of the existence of the gold, they yet wondered if they had won over the last adamant skeptic. They continued to question themselves. Did the state papers bear the signature of authority? Were the old currency accounts accurate? And finally, in order to finance their houses, their vessels, and their land holdings, did the Norwoods make a fortune in trading, smuggling, or privateering, as even some Norwood descendants believed? Going one step further, they photographed and studied the excavated cellar foundation of the log cabin, near where they believed the gold had been found, and where Caleb had lived in that memorable year of 1771.

Then, in what appeared to be of greater significance than all the previous evidence they had gathered, the answer to their questions surfaced one day at the SBHS. In the library archives of this seventy-seven-year-old institution, they found a final genuine proof that the gold had indeed existed. Here they listened to a taped voice message, recorded earlier by a respected elder citizen, Ellen Tufts, who had inherited from her father the Gorham Norwood house. On the tape, Ellen related that she and her twin sister, Edith, were invited by Caleb Norwood's great granddaughter, Susanna Norwood Torrey Tresnon, to view a piece of the gold. For the first time, a direct descendant of Caleb had offered to show her friends one of the legendary gold bars. On the day set to visit their friend, Susanna, Ellen became ill but Edith, having no intention of missing such an opportunity, accepted the invitation. When she returned home she exclaimed excitedly to her sister, 'Tis true! I saw it! I saw a piece of the gold!"

With Ellen's testimony on tape, Don and Peter had at last satisfied their own curiosity about Caleb's cache of gold. Through generations of the Norwood family, and their influence on the development of Cape Ann, and now with the testimony of Ellen Tufts, and with assurance of the gold coming in a direct path from Caleb and Susanna, they had proved beyond a doubt the existence of Caleb's treasure in gold.

The Great Stone Wall had told its story of the Norwood legacy, though myths of pirate gold would go on for more hundreds of years. If the Norwoods had brought their attachment to stone walls with them from England it remained as a constant reminder of that earlier time when the first Francis Norwood came from his British homeland to settle at Cape Ann. It was a fitting place to build a wall, in a community of artists. For stone walls, the two researchers agreed, are a work of art.

BIBLIOGRAPHY

Babson, John J. *History of the Town of Gloucester, Cape Ann: including the Town of Rockport.* Gloucester, Massachusetts: Peter Smith, 1972.

Callam, G. Marion Norwood. *The Norwoods III: A Chronological History*. Bexhill-on-Sea, East Sussex, England: Published by the Author, 1997.

Chamberlain, Allen. *Pigeon Cove: Its Early Settlers and Their Farms, 1702-1840*. [Pigeon Cove, Mass.: Village Improvement Society of Pigeon Cove] Boston: Thomas Todd Co.,

Cooley, John L. *Rockport Sketchbook: Stories of Early Art and Artists.* Rockport, Massachusetts: Rockport Art Association, 1965.

Daggett, John. *A Sketch of the History of Attleborough: From Its Settlement to the Division.* Boston: Press of S.Usher, 1894.

Early Deeds of Essex County. Collection of Cape Ann Historical Society, Gloucester, Massachusetts.

Erkkila, Barbara H. *Hammers on Stone: A History of Cape Ann Granite.* Woolwich, Maine. TBW Books,1980.

Garland, Joseph E. *Guns Off Gloucester.* Gloucester, Massachusetts: Essex County Newspapers, 1975.

Genealogical Sources in the Phillips Library, Peabody-Essex Museum, Salem, Massachusetts.

Giles, Jason. *Ye Headlands of Cape Ann.* Rockport, Massachusetts: Self-published, printed by The Rockport Review, 1900. Collection of Sandy Bay Historical Society and Museums.

History of the Town of Rockport: as comprised in the centennial address of Lemuel Gott, M.D., extracts from the memoranda of Ebenezer Pool, Esq., and interesting items from other sources. compiled by Marshall, John W. et al. Rockport, Massachusetts: 1888.

History of Essex County, Volume II. Compiled by D. Hamilton Hurd. Philadelphia: J.W. Lewis and Company, 1888. Collection of Sandy Bay Historical Society and Museums.

Leckhampton Local History Society. http://www.geocities.com./llhsgl53/.

Leonard, Henry C. *Pigeon Cove and Vicinity.* Boston: F. A. Searle, 1873.

Marshall, J. W. (d. 1889). John White Marshall Papers. Unpublished manuscript. Rockport, Massachusetts: Collection of Sandy Bay Historical Society and Museums.

Massachusetts Archives, Boston, Massachusetts. Comeau, Michael, Head Archivist. Treasurer-Receiver General Records 1775-1784 and Probate Records for Essex County.

McLane, Merrill. *Universalist Papers.* Unpublished manuscript, 2002. Collection of Sandy Bay Historical Society and Museums.

Miller, Eric. *Leckhampton Court: Manor House to Hospice.* Leids, U.K.: Matador, 2002.

Morison, Samuel Eliot. *The Oxford History of the American People*. New York: Oxford University Press, 1965.

Norwood, Maureen. *Frances Norwood, Immigrant to Massachusetts: and His Descendants, 1635-1987*. Baltimore: Gateway Press, 1987.

Norwoods of Leckhampton: Guidance Notes. http://www.geocities.com./llhsgl53norwoods.htm

Parsons, Eleanor C. *Thachers: Island of the Twin Lights*. Canaan, New Hampshire: Phoenix Publishing, 1985.

Perley, Sidney. *The Indian Land Titles of Essex County, Massachusetts*. Salem, Massachusetts:Essex Book and Print Club Publications, no. 3, 1912.

Pool, Ebenezer. *Ebenezer Pool Papers: Volumes I - VI: 1822-1870.* Original manuscripts. Rockport, Massachusetts: Collection of Sandy Bay Historical Society and Museums.

Pringle, James R. *History of the Town and City of Gloucester, Cape Ann, Massachusetts.* [G.H.and W.A. Nichols, Printers, 1892.] Gloucester, Massachusetts: Ten Pound Book Company, 1997.

Registry of Deeds, Essex County. Salem Massachusetts.

Sandy Bay Pier Company Records. Collection of Sandy Bay Historical Society and Museums.

Selectmen's Records. Gloucester Archives, City Hall, Gloucester, Massachusetts.

Solly, George W. *Alluring Rockport: an Unspoiled New England Town on Cape Ann.* Manchester, Massachusetts: North Shore Press, 1924.

Swan, Marshall W. S. *Town on Sandy Bay: a History of Rockport, Massachusetts*. Canaan, New Hampshire: Phoenix Publishing, 1980.

Tagney, Ronald N. *The World Turned Upside Down: Essex County During America's Turbulent Years, 1763-1790*. West Newbury, Massachusetts: Essex County History, 1989.

Thornton, J. Wingate. *Landing at Cape Anne; or the First Charter and Colonial History 1624-1628*. Boston: Gould and Lincoln: 1854. Collection of Sandy Bay Historical Society and Museums.

Thorson, Robert M. *Stone by Stone: The Magnificent History in New England's Stone Walls*. New York: Walker and Company, 2002.

Vital Records of Attleborough Massachusetts to the End of the Year 1849. Salem, Massachusetts: The Essex Institute, 1934.

Williams, Thomas P. "Some Old Houses of Pigeon Cove Massachusetts." *Pencil Points*, August 1933, Volume XIX No. 3. New York.

Young, Alexander. *Chronicles of the First Planters of the Colony Of Massachusetts Bay, from 1623-1636*. Boston: C. C. Little and J. Brown, 1846.

Zacks, Richard. *The Pirate Hunter: the True Story of Captain Kidd.* New York: Hyperion Books, 2002.

INDEX

S

T

W